SHACKLED

A TALE OF WRONGED KIDS, ROGUE JUDGES, AND A TOWN THAT LOOKED AWAY

CANDY J. COOPER

CALKINS CREEK
AN IMPRINT OF ASTRA BOOKS FOR YOUNG READERS
New York

TO BOB
AND TO MY FATHER

For information about permission to reproduce selections from this book,
please contact permissions@astrapublishinghouse.com.

Calkins Creek
An imprint of Astra Books for Young Readers, a division of Astra Publishing House
astrapublishinghouse.com
Printed in the United States of America

ISBN: 978-1-6626-2013-3 (hc)
ISBN: 978-1-6626-2014-0 (eBook)

Library of Congress Cataloging-in-Publication Data
Names: Cooper, Candy J., 1955- author.
Title: Shackled : a tale of wronged kids, rogue judges, and a town that looked away /
   Candy J. Cooper.
Description: First edition. | New York : Calkins Creek, 2024. | Includes bibliographical
   references. | Audience: Grades 7-9 | Summary: "Here is the explosive story of the Kids for
   Cash scandal in Pennsylvania, a judicial justice miscarriage that sent more than 2,500
   children and teens to a for-profit detention center while two judges lined their pockets with
   cash, as told by Candy J. Cooper, an award-winning journalist and Pulitzer Prize finalist"—
   Provided by publisher.
Identifiers: LCCN 2023044554 (print) | LCCN 2023044555 (ebook) |
   ISBN 9781662620133 (hardcover) | ISBN 9781662620140 (ebook)
Subjects: LCSH: Juvenile justice, Administration of—Corrupt practices—Pennsylvania—Juvenile
   literature. | Corruption—Law and legislation—Pennsylvania—Juvenile literature. | Bribery—Law
   and legislation--Pennsylvania—Juvenile literature. | Judicial error—Pennsylvania—Juvenile
   literature. | Juvenile courts—Pennsylvania—Juvenile literature. | Juvenile detention—
   Pennsylvania—Juvenile literature.
Classification: LCC KFP595 .C66 2024 (print) | LCC KFP595 (ebook) | DDC 364.1/34—
   dc23/eng/20231002
LC record available at https://lccn.loc.gov/2023044554
LC ebook record available at https://lccn.loc.gov/2023044555

First edition

10 9 8 7 6 5 4 3 2 1

Design by Carol Bobolts/Red Herring Design
The text is set in ITC Mendoza Roman.
The titles are set in Nexa Rust Sans.

ABANDON ALL HOPE, YE WHO ENTER HERE!

—DANTE ALIGHIERI (1265–1321),
FROM HIS *INFERNO*

CONTENTS

Historians call the Luzerne County Courthouse, set on the banks of the Susquehanna River in Wilkes-Barre, Pennsylvania, an architectural and historical marvel.

CHAPTER 1

PORTAL TO CALAMITY

Sneering insults uttered by a judge, the rattle of leg irons across a floor, the stricken cries of a mother whose child is led away: here was a juvenile courtroom turned into a chamber of cruelty. Carisa Tomkiel, unformed and childlike at fourteen, would later remember the hard, wooden courthouse bench and her building sense of dread on that winter morning in 2005 in downtown Wilkes-Barre. She had looked around the hallway to see her accusers staring at her. She had heard the judge was hard-nosed and sent every person away. She tried to recall her parents' advice: yes, it was wrong to scribble in Magic Marker on a couple of street signs. But it had been a minor childish stunt, and Carisa was a good kid. It was a first offense. If she took responsibility, if she was straightforward and honest and spoke to the judge with a respectful "Yes, sir" and "No, sir," justice would prevail. She would likely be placed on probation, required to clean up the signs or abide by a curfew.

Carisa's parents, who sat nearby, tuned in to the rhythms of the juvenile court. Like others there that winter day, they noticed the lightning speed of the proceedings. Families filed in and out of the courtroom within a period of a minute or two, as if picking up a single grocery item from the Quik Mart. And most

After Carisa Tomkiel and her best friend scribbled silly words on a few street signs in West Pittston, in northeastern Pennsylvania, the young teens were judged delinquent, sentenced to a wilderness boot camp, and led out of a juvenile courtroom in handcuffs and leg irons. Once released, Tomkiel was placed on house arrest for a month and then wore an ankle monitor to school. The ordeal, she said, "broke my brain."

concerning: while each family cluster filed into the courtroom together, only the parents walked out.

Where had the children gone?

∞∞∞

Inside, children and young adults disappeared. Thousands of youths, from all corners of rolling Luzerne County in the coal-ravaged northeastern corner of Pennsylvania, passed through that courtroom door and then vanished through another portal. In between they faced a judge, Mark Ciavarella, who presided over the juvenile court of the county throughout the 2000s. He was known widely as a hanging judge, elected on a platform of zero-tolerance justice, or the idea that people, even children, deserved the harshest penalties for the most trivial mistakes. Short in stature at five foot six, trim and middle-aged with a cap of gray hair, he wore the power uniform of the court—a black judge's robe over a shirt and tie, at times set off with a colorful sports cap. His inscrutable gaze was framed by rectangular, wire-rimmed spectacles that darkened in the sun. His pursed mouth was set in pouchy jowls, and witnesses said he sat on two phone books to elevate himself. Some found the county judge loquacious and personable. Many favored his severe, if paradoxical, approach to caring for kids. They signed on to his unyielding, old-school brand of justice.

∞∞∞

Carisa had dressed up, wearing a stiff white blouse, dress pants, and chunky heels. Her mother had straightened her shoulder-length blond hair for the hearing. In the eighth grade, Carisa was an A and B student who had taught herself the clarinet in order to play in the school band. She had a best friend, Angelia, and the two were like sisters, creating their own private subculture in the dog-eat-dog hierarchy of middle school. They spent time at each other's houses playing *DanceDanceRevolution* on PlayStation 2 or watching *SpongeBob SquarePants* cartoons. Angelia, an A student and two-time student of the month, waited nearby in the hallway of the courthouse with her mother.

Carisa wondered whether she would have a chance to explain to the court what had happened. The two girls, who liked to draw, had watched a *SpongeBob* episode about turning drawings into animated life. They had taken to doodling on paper, on each other's notebooks, or right on their skin. Water-based markers washed off too quickly, so the young women found Sharpies to draw indelible watches around their wrists. And in the fall of 2004, in the midst of an explosion of graffiti appearing on nearly every public park bench, abandoned building, and playground slide in their town, the girls used their Sharpies to draw on a few street signs. To a Watch for Children sign they added, underneath, "*For Michael Jackson.*" On a stop sign they wrote, "*Go Bush.*" They thought it was funny. The scribbles were "just silly things," Angelia later explained under oath. "Very childish things, nothing bad. Nothing gang like."

But the rash of spray-painted graffiti around town had prompted citizen complaints and then a crackdown by local police. A classmate, while out tagging, was caught. And when police questioned him, he blamed all of the town graffiti—the bright, bold spray-painting of gang symbols, the crude drawings of genitalia, the lewd phrases—on Carisa and Angelia, the low-key duo who had little social clout at school. Soon a police officer was calling the parents of Carisa and Angelia to let them know the girls would be charged with eighty-six counts of vandalism and institutional vandalism, or essentially every instance of graffiti defacing the town of West Pittston. A ridiculous claim, Carisa first thought. But several other classmates had signed affidavits accusing Carisa and Angelia of all charges, and those girls were also milling about the court hallway now. A councilperson was there to testify against them, too. Carisa's stomach lurched, as if she were climbing the steepest rise of the world's tallest roller coaster, minus that weightless thrill on the way down. She just wanted the moment to end.

◑◑◑

Carisa and Angelia were but two. Many thousands of youths appeared before Judge Ciavarella during his time on the court from 1996 to 2009, entering one courtroom door, disappearing through another. In between, the man in the robe redirected young lives like a sorting wizard, with a booming voice and a stream of schoolyard sneers and put-downs. "Shut up," he ordered the mother of a teen he was jailing, threatening to lock her up, too. "You sit down and you shut up!" he snapped at a substance abuse counselor defending a first-time offender in a marijuana case. "What makes you think you can do this kind of crap?" he yelled at a teenager at the start of her hearing.

He turned his courtroom into spectacle. The hearings by state law should have been closed, yet field trips of twenty to twenty-five schoolchildren jammed into the courtroom jury box to watch the drama. Teachers made arrangements with the judge personally for the tours as warnings to their students. The longtime chief of juvenile probation later remarked on the quickness of the hearings. "Zip, zip," she said. "That was it." The judge, after all, often heard twenty cases in a single morning, and court workers said he sometimes mentioned an afternoon tee time at the golf club.

The same probation chief described courtroom "antics," including Ciavarella's irrepressible passion for organized sports, interwoven with the serious business of juvenile justice. Wearing a NASCAR hat on the bench, with nervous families before him, Ciavarella paused proceedings to collect sports wagers from courtroom workers. "And then in the next breath conducting a hearing and sending their child away," said the juvenile probation chief, Sandra Brulo, under oath. "I had a lot of concern about that." The judge asked one young woman which team she favored in a baseball game. She chose the wrong team, in his view, so he sent her back to detention for another six months. On another day, because he was in a good mood, Ciavarella sent a fifteen-year-old home. "He let me go because he won a bet [on] a football game," she later recalled. "He was feeling nice he said."

∞

On that cold day in 2005, the chaotic atmosphere in the low-ceilinged courtroom at Penn Place, a flat-roofed, flat-sided, brick behemoth in downtown Wilkes-Barre, promised anything but mercy. Carisa and Angelia stood before Ciavarella with their parents and a lawyer in a hearing that played out like a kangaroo court. The adult witness, the councilman, was unable to identify Carisa or Angelia. The remaining statements were deemed hearsay. The judge was highly distracted, and Angelia's mother later described the experience, from the moment of her daughter's arrest, as "such a crazy case" because she had been forewarned, actually threatened by the arresting police officer, that a football game might determine the girls' fate.

"The officer had told us that if she [Angelia] didn't plead guilty to every single charge," she later said under oath, "that he was going to make sure [she] got to see Judge Ciavarella on a day that Penn State had lost the previous weekend, because Judge Ciavarella will send all of them to jail if Penn State loses."

And Carisa, too, later remembered that Ciavarella chatted idly with others in the courtroom about possible game outcomes. "It could've been a Penn Super Bowl that year if the Steelers played the Eagles," was the gist of the conversation, she later remembered. "He went off topic and started shooting the breeze with other cops there and bailiffs or whoever they were."

Angelia later recalled that "I didn't feel like it was taken very seriously at all. So instead of listening to our case we were talking about football."

∞

And yet, no matter how unfitting or incorrect the judge's banter, how degrading the remarks, how senseless the rulings, a gaping silence hung over the courtroom, a strange indifference, a mass act of *complicity* seized the many dozens of professional adults who milled about in the business-as-usual atmosphere akin to a bustling marketplace. These silent witnesses included probation and police officers, social workers, court reporters, and the judge's administrative staff. Also present were members of the Pennsylvania bar, including assistant district attorneys, public defenders, and local private defense attorneys—all sworn to uphold laws that protect children and youth and to report infractions that might harm them.

No one objected when Ciavarella instituted a drill. As families stepped off a third-floor elevator, they were met by a probation worker sitting behind a table. The worker's job was to persuade an accused youth and "advising adult" to sign a form or "waiver of counsel." By signing, the family agreed to give up all rights to a lawyer, either one they paid for or one the court appointed. Many youths and families signed without a thought, as if signing in at a doctor's office, or simply stating what was at that moment true—they did not *have* a lawyer. It didn't mean they didn't *want* one.

The waiver helped court proceedings move swiftly. But it violated the law, which in Pennsylvania required a judge to conduct an out-loud, in-court, face-to-face, on-the-record conversation with a young defendant known as a "colloquy," so that the accused youth fully understood the unfamiliar legal words that described the rights they would give up by facing the judge alone. That clerk at the elevator with the written waiver, it turned out, was a trick.

The result was that more than half of child defendants faced the judge alone, left to interpret a load of legal jargon foreign to their ears. What was that waiver, anyway? What did it mean, legally, to admit to being guilty? Most adults didn't understand the law school words pinging around the courtroom. Children certainly did not. But lawyers did.

Many juvenile courtrooms refuse to allow children and youths to appear in court without lawyers. But Ciavarella's courtroom used the clerk with the waiver. And without legal counsel, most children skipped straight to pleading "guilty," thinking it might soften the judge and lessen their punishment. But admitting to guilt meant giving up the right to a trial where a child might present evidence of good character, high grades, college prospects. It meant giving up the right to question witnesses who might be lying, or to call experts who could put the child's behavior into context by describing, say, an abusive home life, or the death of a parent, or family poverty, and how best to help.

Instead, families signed the waiver and handed their fate to the judge. The judge sent the children through the mystery door.

⊂⊃⊃

Carisa and Angelia listened as Ciavarella judged the two girls "delinquent," or guilty, of eighty-six counts of vandalism. In the next breath he imposed their sentence: an indefinite stay at a wilderness camp that relied on extreme discipline and boot camp-like drills. With those words the girls heard a rattling sound from a corner of the courtroom. Soon a court worker appeared holding two medieval-looking sets of shackles. The worker enchained Carisa and Angelia like cartoon criminals—wrapping heavy leather belts around their narrow waists; snapping iron handcuffs to their child-size wrists; and clamping leg irons around their slender ankles. The girls looked to their stunned parents. The court worker turned the girls away. Ciavarella called the next case. The girls clomped in their high-heeled dress shoes past the judge's bench and toward the door.

Carisa felt a terror that lodged in her gut. Where were they going? Why were they in chains and stumbling away from their families? It was as if she and Angelia were murderers, not sign scribblers.

The girls were led into a stuffy cell-like room and fastened to a metal bench with other shackled children. Back in the courtroom, Angelia's mother panicked. She ran out the door and to the probation department to explain that her daughter was an epileptic and needed close medical supervision. She had not expected that Angelia would be sent from the courtroom directly to a far-flung wilderness program. She needed to go home to pick up her daughter's medication.

"Nope," the head of probation told her, "she has to go now."

"But you don't understand," Angelia's mother pleaded. "If you don't let her take her medicine she will go into a seizure."

Later that morning Carisa and Angelia were led, handcuffed, to a transport where a driver planted Angelia in a back seat and Carisa in the passenger seat and insisted on silence. Carisa had never been away from home before. The car hurtled past long stretches of gray monotone rural winter scenery and Carisa wondered, Was this New York? New Jersey? Still Pennsylvania?

ᏅᏅᏅ

An impressive range of investigating experts would later probe how or why Carisa and Angelia's story repeated itself day after day over the course of more than five years in the early 2000s in Luzerne County. Why did a community let a judge enchain and detain its children and youth over childish and youthful misdoings? Why did professionals watch and say nothing? Researchers have studied silence throughout history, as well as the horrors that can unfold when witnesses look away.

Yet what professionals ignored and experts later decried, some parents felt almost instantly. Something *was* wrong. Carisa's mother, Andrea Tomkiel, knew that much as she watched Carisa and Angelia shuffle out of the courtroom, dragging their irons across the floor like child ghosts in a horror movie.

"You guys are all corrupt!" Andrea Tomkiel shouted at Ciavarella. The courtroom broke into applause. The judge threatened to jail Andrea Tomkiel for ninety days. Her lawyer tried to silence her. Her husband had warned her about standing up to authority.

"You're crooked!" she called out anyway, "every one of you!"

CHAPTER 2

JUST GREED

A leap roughly fifty years backward in time, to a catastrophic coal mine collapse underground, offers clues to an early 2000s juvenile courtroom gone awry. Certain threads run through nearly a century of life in the Wyoming Valley, a bowl of a region in northeastern Pennsylvania marked today by scarred mountains and abandoned-storefront towns. In this corner of the world, history unfolds as a cycle in overlapping parts: greed, corruption, silence, tragedy, and suffering. Economic inequality underlies all, and the cycle spins from underground coal mines to above-ground courthouses, from men and boys of the past to thousands of children and youth still suffering today.

That earlier disaster, in the winter of 1959, began on a day when dozens of coalminers toiled underground at the River Slope

Mine at Port Griffith, northeast of Wilkes-Barre. The mighty Susquehanna River rushed just overhead, its waters dripping and drizzling down the mine's timbered walls. A worker hung up his heavy winter coat in the morning only to find it covered in icicles by day's end. Many knew they were close to the earth's surface when they felt the passing rumble of the Lehigh Valley Railroad.

The heavily leaking river led to premonitions among some coalminers working for the law-bending Knox Coal Company. One man told his foreman "something's wrong" with the coal path he was chiseling overhead. He might have been carving too close to the waterway. The foreman in turn talked to his crew about escape plans and marked an exit route with chalk. Another miner had a recurring nightmare in which his bedroom ceiling collapsed on top of him and his young son as they slept. And an electrician working in the mine shared with his sister: "One of these days we are all going to die with our boots on like rats in a trap."

In late January of 1959, an unusual warming trend began to melt the frozen Susquehanna, causing icebergs as large as refrigerators to break off and rush downstream. The river's crest rose twenty feet in three days. At the River Slope Mine, the Knox Coal Company was excavating coal illegally. Instead of chipping away more or less parallel to the shoreline, as mining maps and safety regulations required, Knox had followed the thick vein of dark black coal wherever it went. It led coalminers to turn at a right angle, violate the mapped stop lines drawn by engineers, and follow the coal seam out under the riverbed. The men carved, blasted, and burrowed through rock for many hundreds of feet out, inching upward and ever closer to the river bottom.

In the late morning of January 22, two miners working in the upper reaches of the mine heard a shrill cracking and screeching sound emanating from the ceiling. The men summoned the assistant foreman, John Williams, who had been talking with three other workers blasting out rock in a deeper bed below. Williams excused himself, climbed the passage, and stepped into a side chamber to examine the apparently splintering timbers above. All at once a thunderous crack gave way to a spectacular tidal wave of rock, ice, timbers, debris, and tons and tons of water.

⊖⊖⊖

Usually a lust for diamonds, land, power, or fame starts wars and ruins people and nations. In northeastern Pennsylvania conflict derived from a piece of black rock. The hard, shiny coal known as anthracite was considered the highest quality coal in the world because its flame is lower and cleaner-burning than the softer, dirtier, and more widely available bituminous. The largest deposit of anthracite coal anywhere lies within about five hundred square miles across five counties of northeastern Pennsylvania. The northernmost field of that deposit, shaped like a handlebar mustache, stretches across Luzerne County, part of the isolated valley surrounded by mountain ridges, about 128 miles west of New York City, on the far side of the Pocono Mountains. The north branch of the Susquehanna flows through the region, and the county seat, Wilkes-Barre, was once described by a state supreme court justice as the most picturesquely beautiful spot in Pennsylvania.

Crime writers and historians, on the other hand, have described the area as a place where corruption is as much a part of the landscape as the denuded lands, polluted rivers, and hills of coal waste all around. "The entire region," wrote Matt Birkbeck, an author of two biographies of organized crime figures who lived and operated in the anthracite region, "from Scranton to Wilkes-Barre, had long been thought to have operated in its own vacuum, where the crooks were the good guys and everyone else looked the other way." An historian of northeastern Pennsylvania calls his homeland The Wild East.

But coal came first, arising from shifting tectonic plates, then a twisting and folding of earth into ridges and mountains, and finally a compression of underground swampland that alchemized into anthracite. Above ground, the terrain was so rugged it discouraged Native Americans from settling in the forested core of the region. The Lenape lived in small tribes along the Delaware River to the east, and the Susquehannocks inhabited the northern part of the valley. Some evidence shows anthracite's first use as a black paint on rock.

Its first use in manufacturing is credited to a Wilkes-Barre blacksmith who burned anthracite for his forge in the 1760s. In the early nineteenth century, with the depletion of forests near urban centers, industrialists looked to anthracite for commercial uses, seeking ways to burn the rock as fuel on a large scale. Gradually anthracite became known, in Philadelphia and New York, as a clean alternative to charcoal for home heating. In the mid- to late 1800s, railroad titans found a way to move and transport anthracite into the center of American commerce. In addition to heating homes, anthracite began to feed steel mills and to power ships and trains, becoming the literal fuel for the American move toward mass production, the industrial revolution. Anthracite, historians later said, turned America into a world superpower.

Small coal companies soon consolidated into larger ones. King Coal, as it was called, generated fabulous wealth for those who owned and operated the coal mines and built the railroads that took the coal to market. But coal's great prosperity relied on terrible hardship for the workers who mined the sediment underground. Coal barons lived in splendor in Victorian estates, and then erected shabby housing for immigrant mine workers near the entrances to mines. These company towns, known as coal patches, looked like fragile clusters of rickety frame houses and included a school and a company store, which often charged outrageous prices and held a monopoly on all of the goods and groceries coal miners needed to survive.

At work, coal miners faced the everyday possibilities of maiming, drowning, and being buried alive. They descended deep into a black hell, as some called it, or the total blackness of earth, sometimes miles underground and below the water table. They carved and dynamited miles of horizontal tunnels to access the shiny seams of black coal compressed between layers of rock. They worked in strained positions, squeezing into narrow passages and lying all day on their backs or stomachs. They labored alongside huge colonies of rats, which would eat or drag away nearly anything left untended by a miner, from a set of false teeth to a whole lunchbox. The mines were also notorious for poor ventilation, exposing miners to deadly fumes that could lead to asphyxiation and explosions. Coal dust settled in folds of skin and stained eyebrows black, and later lodged in lungs to be coughed up through the night. Many miners died of black lung disease.

Miners put in fourteen-hour days for starvation wages, often forcing their young sons into the mines. Preadolescent "breaker boys" sorted chunks of coal as it dropped down a conveyor, while "spraggers" were boys who slowed the speed of coal cars by thrusting sticks into the wheels. They wore bandannas and chewed tobacco in order to keep coal dust from their lungs.

"Breaker boys" were young men between the ages of 8 and 12 employed in the anthracite coal mines in northeastern Pennsylvania during the latter half of the 19th century. They worked 10-hour days, 6 days a week, sitting on wooden seats, legs straddled, while hovering over conveyor belts. They picked through chunks of rock, separating anthracite from slate and other impurities before the coal went to market. The practice of using children in coal mining ended in 1908.

Death was a constant: "A husband, or son, or father, leaves home in the morning in perfect health," wrote historian Peter Roberts, in a 1901 textbook on coal mining, "and in a few hours is brought home a corpse." Death and disaster were so common in the mines, Roberts added, that few even spoke of it.

Disaster struck everywhere in Luzerne County: An 1869 fire in the Avondale Colliery killed one hundred ten men and boys. A rush of water and quicksand in December of 1885 at a Nanticoke mine drowned and encased fifty-eight miners. And an explosion in 1919 at the Baltimore Mine Tunnel in Wilkes-Barre killed ninety-two people.

The massive number of injuries, deaths, and catastrophes gave rise to labor unions to protect the workers. By the mid-1890s, the United Mine Workers of America had sprung up in the region, advocating livable wages and safe working conditions in the mines. In places where the unions were held off, mine workers went on strike and shut down the mines.

Immense conflict erupted between coal operators and miners, between union and nonunion workers. There were bombings and assassinations. Coal companies hired private security forces and law enforcement fortified their ranks with untrained citizens. One flashpoint occurred in 1897 in a Luzerne County town called Lattimer, where four hundred unarmed protesting miners carrying an American flag were met by the Luzerne County sheriff and a posse of 150 hired men, all pointing Winchester rifles. The shooters mowed down the workers as they fled, killing nineteen and injuring thirty-eight, nearly all of the workers shot in the back.

The strikes and shutdowns in the coalfields soon took their toll on coal supplies, strangling sources of fuel as well as profits for coal titans. A famous 1902 strike drew elected officials and finally President Theodore Roosevelt before it was settled, giving miners more protections.

But Big Coal's losses, along with the country's turn toward oil, gas, and electricity, drove the industry toward a new model of mining. The largest coal companies began subleasing to small-fry operators to mine the coal and manage workers and messy labor issues. Safety, in this new arrangement, fell away as the small rogue subleasers, acting like bootleggers, "wanted to do what the hell they wanted to do," a coal company official later said.

The Knox Coal Company was one such small independent contractor, and it subleased from one of the big five in the region, the Pennsylvania Coal Company. The crooked operations of small Knox were well known to big Pennsylvania Coal—and even considered advantageous, since Knox's law-breaking promised more coal and greater profits. The big company, then, looked the other way as unscrupulous Knox began mining far afield of where mining was allowed.

The general loosening of standards in turn increased opportunities for organized crime to sweep in and gain a foothold in the anthracite industry. Hundreds of thousands of immigrants had discovered mining in Pennsylvania after working in mines in their home countries all across Europe—in Wales, Germany, Scotland, and Italy. Some had worked in sulfur mines around Sicily, many of them run by organized crime. Looking to escape mob-run mining, many upstanding Sicilians found their way to Pennsylvania and filled jobs in every facet of the industry. But organized crime found its way, too, and by the early to mid-1930s, the American Mafia had assumed a powerful influence over anthracite. People knew of its tightening grip but did not speak of it. "No one really commented on it," one of the last surviving officers of the Pennsylvania Coal Company said in a 1992 interview. "I suppose it was probably well known throughout the region and everything, but you just kept your mouth shut or you were in big trouble."

Generations of Mafia bosses became active in anthracite over the decades, with names like Santo "King of the Night" Volpe, Joseph "Joe the Barber" Barbara, and Russell "The Quiet Don" Bufalino. When Bufalino died in 1994, his longstanding protégée, driver, and bodyguard, William "Big Billy" D'Elia, took over the Bufalino crime family. As anthracite mining died off, organized crime lived on, worming its way into the garment industry, state gambling operations, and finally through the back doors of municipal government, including the Luzerne County Courthouse.

The lawlessness meant bribery and corruption flourished in the mines, as companies paid off union leaders to pass weak contracts and bribed government inspectors to simply stay away. "[The inspectors] didn't even go inside [the mines]," said one miner, Joe Costa, who worked for the Knox Coal Company. He was interviewed in 1992 by the authors of *The Knox Mine Disaster*, Robert P. Wolensky, Kenneth C. Wolensky, and Nicole H. Wolensky. Costa continued, "[They] just filled out the papers. I remember [a Knox boss] said to me, 'Joe, here's a hundred dollars. Take the mine inspector out and show him a good time.' So I took him fishing and we went out."

One dangerous trick of the subleasers was to scavenge already-excavated and abandoned mines for leftover coal. They "robbed the pillars," which meant stripping the old mines of the thick columns of coal left behind to prop up walls and roofs to prevent collapse. By early 1959 at the River Slope Mine, the Knox Coal Company had blasted the pillars nearly out of existence.

⊂⊃⊂

The weakened pillars were but one of the well-known and ignored hazards leading to that January morning in 1959, when Assistant Foreman John Williams rushed toward the shrill cracking and splintering sounds in the timbers overhead. By then no one had measured how closely the miners had scraped to the riverbed. Regulations called for a fifty-foot thickness; Knox had negotiated a thirty-five-foot divide. But the heedless company had scraped to within nineteen inches of the river bottom—a hairbreadth in mining terms, a tissue holding back an angry, ice-laden river.

"I no more than put my foot in the place and looked up than the roof gave way," Williams later told investigators.

Williams and another laborer sprinted up the slope while a third man, Frank Domoracki, stopped, turned, and looked to the lower vein where the three rock men had been drilling to lengthen that bed. The water, seeking its lowest point, gushed past him as he hollered, "Get out! The river broke in!"

As he spoke, the black water swallowed up the lower passage and Domoracki spun around and raced up the slope, crying out to an engineer on his way: "Get everybody out of the May Shaft and shut off the power because the river broke in. Tiny and his two buddies are drowned."

The engineer called a superintendent, who alerted the men underground to evacuate, though he didn't say why. Unaware of the urgency, some miners first gathered tools and lunch boxes— a deadly mistake for some. Fear gripped others as the water, filled with car-size icebergs slamming together, roared in their ears and knocked them around. They grabbed on to old, long-dead electrical lines to keep from being swept away.

In the moments that followed, the miners splintered into groups and sloshed toward slopes, elevators, and air shafts as the tidal wave rose. One group found the shaft of an elevator lift but no one aboveground answered their bell-ringing summons. Others, with water to their necks, began swimming against the rushing current. Another group, led by a surveyor with maps, found an abandoned air shaft blocked by roots, garbage, and ice. And yet another cluster of twenty-six men, searching for the same air shaft, missed a turn and wandered for eight hours over many miles underground, lost and terrified.

Eventually, the elevator arrived to hoist thirteen men to safety. Entry to the air shaft was cleared and one wily miner clawed his way fifty feet straight up and ran for help to lift out those behind him, later to win a medal of courage. Rescuers eventually found the twenty-six lost men and got them to safety. One swimmer survived, but when he looked back his weaker coworkers had disappeared.

The hours that followed involved an epic struggle to plug up the enormous whirlpooling funnel of water created by the breakthrough. The hole was sucking billions of gallons of water underground like a giant bathtub drain, with the potential to not only flood and seal up the River Slope Mine, but to fill adjacent mines and destroy them, too. It was a struggle to save lives and a way of life.

Workers cut and bent railroad tracks to hover just above the hole and sent massive loads of materials sailing off the tracks, including many hundreds of coal and train cars that some later called the train to hell. They dumped tons of rock, hay, boulders

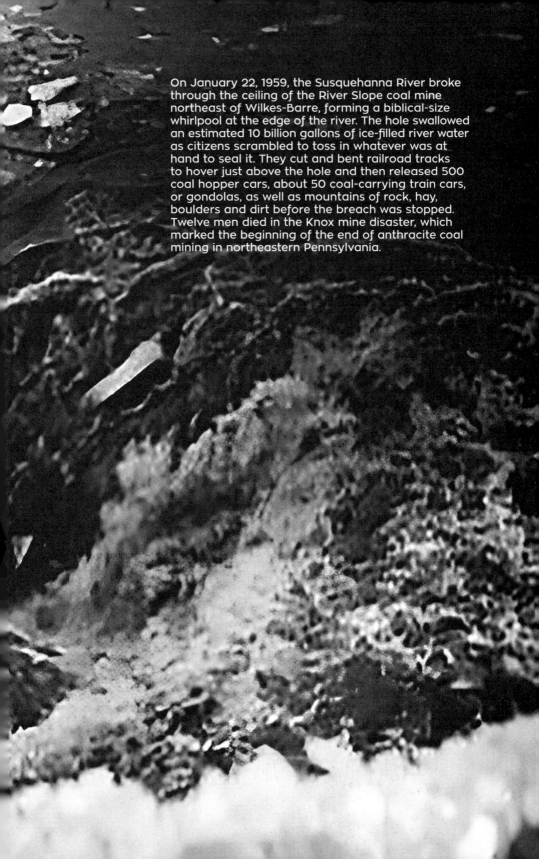

On January 22, 1959, the Susquehanna River broke through the ceiling of the River Slope coal mine northeast of Wilkes-Barre, forming a biblical-size whirlpool at the edge of the river. The hole swallowed an estimated 10 billion gallons of ice-filled river water as citizens scrambled to toss in whatever was at hand to seal it. They cut and bent railroad tracks to hover just above the hole and then released 500 coal hopper cars, about 50 coal-carrying train cars, or gondolas, as well as mountains of rock, hay, boulders and dirt before the breach was stopped. Twelve men died in the Knox mine disaster, which marked the beginning of the end of anthracite coal mining in northeastern Pennsylvania.

and dirt before the hole was sealed. In the spring, engineers diverted the river to seal the gap for good.

And meanwhile, families of the missing watched from hilltops or waited at home. Today the bodies of their loved ones remain entombed underground. In total, twelve men died at Knox— among an estimated thirty-five thousand men who died in the anthracite fields.

"I don't think you should call it the *Knox Mine Disaster*, I think they should call it the *Knox Mine Murders*," said the daughter of one of the victims, Eugene Ostrowski, Sr.

∞

Four investigations after the Knox disaster pointed to weather, negligence, and corruption. Greed proved a powerful motivator, investigators said, as both company and workers who were paid by the weight of their haul stood to profit. One surviving miner, Al Kanaar, reflected on the culture in an oral history project: "That's all, just greed. You can name a book 'Greed' and write forever on it in the anthracite, from the first mines that were ever opened. That's all it was, all the time."

A grand jury found Knox violated labor laws, bribed union leaders, and was originally owned in part by a Mafia kingpin, John Sciandra. "Owners, bosses, inspectors and mineworkers alike knew that illegalities had become epidemic," summarized the Wolensky historians. Everyone knew the coal titans on Wall Street used the smaller companies to accomplish crooked or illegal goals. "They knew that organized crime had become part of the cancer. Finally, they knew that the [union] had turned away from the mineworkers to become an accomplice to the scandal."

The authors added: "Many otherwise upstanding citizens

participated in the crooked dealings. The culture of corruption that had engulfed the industry caused serious damage to the community's social and moral fabric, leaving wounds that remain to the present."

And a 2023 editorial in local newspaper *The Times Leader*, announcing commemorative events related to anthracite history, summarized coal's legacy.

"It shredded our landscape," the newspaper wrote, "killed our fathers and children, and fashioned a new breed of often self-serving business barons. It left a legacy of culm banks and orange acid mine water we continue to combat, and the tragedy of black lung and other life-altering ailments lingering long after the cause vanished."

⚙⚙⚙

Coal's end left a jobs vacuum, as some hundred thousand jobs in the anthracite industry in the early 1900s dropped to just five thousand by 1965. The company-owned coal patches turned into tiny Luzerne County towns—seventy-six municipalities in a mix of cities, boroughs, and townships, each with its own government requiring some combination of mayors, councilpersons, supervisors, school board members, and more.

Municipal jobs became a new center for corruption, with mayors, school superintendents, and other powerful people able to hire and fire at will, offer jobs to friends and family, and insist on paybacks for their favors. "We were under the thumb of coal barons for a long time," said David Sosar, a political science professor at King's College. "What we did is trade coal barons for financial barons and political barons."

Some in the region have lived through that trade. Deborah

Jerock, of Pittston, was a coal miner's daughter. Her father worked a lifetime in the mines and had friends in the Knox disaster. When he was diagnosed with black lung disease he needed insurance. "All you had to do was get an envelope of money and drop it off at [a company boss's] house and that was how you got black lung insurance," Deborah Jerock recalled. Her father got his coverage until his death.

Jerock became a wife and mother, living in the same Luzerne County town where the 1959 disaster had struck. And then, straddling history, Jerock found herself in a juvenile courtroom nearly 45 years later, where her two young children were marched through a door for reasons she did not understand.

CHAPTER 3

INTOLERANCE

April and Robert Jerock were ten and fourteen when they acted on the bad advice of an older boy from their neighborhood. In the summer of 2003, they followed him through the open front door of a Pittston-area house he said had been abandoned. April and Robert grabbed a few board games and ran home. They showed their mother and described some strange items in that house: guns, and a slew of live and dead cats. Deborah Jerock dialed 9-1-1. Soon the police were reprimanding April and Robert for trespassing and stealing. The chastised children returned the games, but three months later they were summoned to the courtroom of Luzerne County Juvenile Court Judge Mark Ciavarella.

A few minutes after that hearing began, the judge pronounced the Jerock children delinquent and sentenced them to detention.

Hearing this, Deborah Jerock fainted on the floor. "Is she ok? Did she die?" the children called out as they stumbled away in handcuffs and leg irons. Robert was learning disabled and emotionally impaired and looked to his younger sister for strength, but April cried, too. The siblings were led to a holding room, fastened to a bench, and ordered to quiet down.

Late in the morning of that fall day in 2003, the Jerock children climbed into a prison van, sped away from the courthouse, veered northeast, and turned thirty minutes later into wooded foothills

Robert and April Jerock, and many thousands of children and youth, were sent by Luzerne County's juvenile court to a new for-profit detention center, Pennsylvania Child Care, built in an industrial park on the outskirts of the county. The youth lockup was managed by Mid-Atlantic Youth Services, another company owned by the same two men who owned the jail. Today the facility is operated by the state for residential treatment for youth.

in the outer reaches of Luzerne County. There in a clear-cut hollow of an industrial park sat a cinderblock building that sprawled for forty-four thousand square feet. It was squat, flat sided, beige, landscaped, and half-encircled by a fence topped with tiers of barbed wire. A sign at the entry looked stenciled by an amateur hand: Mid Atlantic Youth Services, PA Child Care.

Robert and April were led inside the juvenile detention center, where Robert heard the sounds of pounding on metal doors and kid voices echoing through the halls while staff bellowed to keep quiet. Robert later did his own pounding to get out, even to go to the bathroom, where a guard always watched. April was strip-searched and given delousing treatments in her "lady parts." To Robert it felt like a dungeon. Their mother, they learned hours later, was alive—if utterly anguished.

In the front lobby of that kid lockup known as Pennsylvania Child Care, or PA Child Care as the sign says, a laminated notice on the wall spells out a guiding principle. "ZERO" reads the top line, in two-inch red lettering. "TOLERANCE" reads the next, in bold white font.

Zero tolerance is the one-size-fits-all judicial philosophy that swept the country after the April 1999 school shooting at Columbine High School in Littleton, Colorado, that killed twelve children and a teacher. After Columbine, politicians won election on zero-tolerance campaigns. They passed zero-tolerance laws and poured tax dollars into hiring enforcers, or school resource officers, to insure zero tolerance in schools. The media helped popularize the idea of a juvenile crime wave and spread the scary notion of the adolescent "super predator." Officials everywhere sent more and more children to prison.

Zero tolerance defined the Luzerne County Juvenile Court

throughout the early 2000s. That's because its architect, once a troublemaker himself, grew up learning the ways of stiff punishment right at his father's knee.

⊂⊖⊃

Mark Ciavarella came from modest means. He grew up one of three in the working-class East End section of Wilkes-Barre, in a close-knit, Catholic neighborhood, where the church his family attended sat just three doors down from their home. As a boy he earned the nickname "Scooch," adopted from his father, which comes from the Italian *scocciare*, "to pester." He excelled in academics and athletics, once pitching a no-hitter in a Little League baseball game. He went to Catholic high school where, despite his short stature, he helped the school basketball team win a state championship. He attended nearby King's College and went on to earn a law degree from Duquesne University in Pittsburgh. As a practicing lawyer for seventeen years, Ciavarella's young pestering grew into an assertive, even abrasive, manner in the courtroom. He was loud, self-assured, and "just short of being obnoxious," one judge who knew him said.

His harsh manner in turn predicted the theme of his announced run for county judge in 1994. "It's time for people who break the law to realize they'll be punished," he said in declaring his candidacy. Tough love became his campaign theme: "The greatest rehabilitative tool we have is punishment." Drug dealers and sex offenders deserved "the harshest punishment" he could use under Pennsylvania law. "If you violate our rights, you're going to pay," he warned. "You're going to pay dearly." He became a judge in 1996, and his tough-guy approach continued on the bench. Scooch eventually earned a new nickname, Mr. Zero Tolerance.

Before his tenure, the job of juvenile court had been spread among county judges. But once Ciavarella was appointed he gained sole control over the county's juvenile justice system. His number-one goal on the bench was to frighten children, he later said. "I wanted these kids to think that I was the biggest S.O.B. that ever lived," he later told the filmmakers of *Kids for Cash*, a 2013 feature documentary examining the county's court practices. "I wanted them to be scared out of their minds when they had to deal with me." His scared-straight approach would insure that no child would want to return to his courtroom, he said.

In Ciavarella's view, lax parenting caused kids to break rules. It was his job to override the soft, coddling, unbounded style of modern caretaking.

He spoke at school assemblies across the county warning students that if they misbehaved, he would lock them up. A schoolyard fight or smoking on school grounds would lead to automatic detention in his rulebook. And community leaders embraced the crackdown. School officials, especially, began to use Ciavarella to get rid of troublemakers. Police chiefs and school resource officers drew up more petitions to send kids to juvenile court. Parents of the well-behaved believed their children were safer. A community, in short, signed on. And Ciavarella made a point of reading aloud letters from satisfied parents in the courtroom. "Everybody loved it," the chief public defender later said. A school administrator praised Ciavarella in a letter to the editor, saying he was "always fair and firm." The judge "created a bond of trust and confidence" with youths, the letter writer said, adding: "His concern for their well being after adjudication is what makes him so special."

His staff later described the juvenile judge as a good man

who treated them like family and wanted the best for the youth in his courtroom, offering hugs and encouragement in sidebar meetings. Others noted his visits to detention halls, kid sporting events, and high school graduations. He served for nearly twenty years as solicitor for a Catholic youth center. And in 2006 Ciavarella was named "Man of the Year" by the Greater Wilkes-Barre Friendly Sons of St. Patrick. Neighbors who had watched the young Ciavarella grow up praised their local boy's exceptional rise. They said he visited the old neighborhood every day to check on his aging parents until their passing.

And Ciavarella boasted that his stern methods really worked. He said juvenile recidivism rates in Luzerne County—the number of children re-offending and returning to lockup—dropped dramatically during his tenure. Experts later said those numbers merely reflected locking up too many kids for too long. Youths could hardly re-offend while they were in jail.

ᗑᗏᗋ

Despite the judge's misleading data and his strong public support, social science research was at the same time exposing the profound and lasting harms of placing nonviolent young people under lock and key. Studies showed that ripping children from home, even for a few days, can lead to profound trauma in the short and long term. Longitudinal studies of children in detention showed harms in adulthood by nearly any measure, from school performance to employment success to emotional maturity, psychological well-being, and criminal behavior. Imprisoning kids stunted their growth and robbed them of the trial and error of making decisions and mistakes—the building blocks of becoming autonomous adults. And dropping children into a criminal subculture was like lowering them into a lion's maw. Once locked up, young detainees were cut off from the supports of school, family, work, or community. Kid prison was like crime school, and to survive it, kids studied that world. They formed alliances. Once released, they were physically freed but often psychologically stuck in a delinquent identity that followed them into adulthood, leading straight to the doors of adult prison.

Researchers were also learning that successful outcomes among nonviolent young people favored appropriate consequences, but guided by fairness and support. Children were more likely to succeed if they and their families stayed together and received services targeted to the underlying problems that may have led to the misbehavior. Those findings began to strongly influence policy across the country. The practice of sending kids to lockup slowed dramatically. Juvenile detention centers closed, and the graph lines tracking the numbers of both youth in confinement and detention centers dropped precipitously. New models took their place, including in Pennsylvania, which introduced a groundbreaking "restorative justice" model in the late 1990s. It emphasized addressing conflicts within families and communities. Ciavarella didn't care for it.

With no special knowledge or training in juvenile law, Ciavarella's methods derived more from his own family history, he later said. His boyhood offenses had been arguably more serious than those of the children and youths he later sent to lockup. He had gotten in fights for which he was suspended a few times in high school. He was caught by police trying to steal a car. If as a judge he had faced his young self, he would certainly have sent himself to juvenile detention.

But his parents acted as his judge and jury. His father, who worked at a brewery, and his mother, a telephone operator, had been loving and caring but firm, he later explained. He had needed no judge or courtroom to learn right from wrong. His father's heavy hand had done the job.

"My father was very hot-tempered, easy to fly off the handle," he recalled in the *Kids for Cash* documentary.

"I was a freshman or sophomore in high school. And we drank a couple quarts of beer one night. One friend said, 'Why don't we take that car and go for a joy ride?' As we were about to get in the car I heard this voice say, 'What are you doing?'

"I see my cousin and my friend take off.

"The police officer says to me, 'You better come with me.' The next thing I know the juvenile detective . . . said he'd give me a ride home. And as we're driving to East End, I'm getting sicker and sicker and sicker.

"We walk in the house. My mother calls my father. And he said to me, 'What's the problem here?'

"I looked at my father and I said, 'We were going to steal.' And I didn't get the word out of my mouth.

"And he just looks at me and he says to me, 'Look at your mother.' And she was just hysterical. And she kept saying, 'I can't believe my son's a criminal.'

"At which point in time my father, he starts to wind up, and I know it's coming. And he hits me and knocks me out cold."

ᴑᴔᴑ

Amateur psychology might ask whether the brutality of a father could predict a son's sadistic turn. But then again, after Ciavarella was on the bench for a few years, he took up a cause that looked like the crusade of a man who cared. The judge said children were suffering in the county's old youth jail. The rundown 1930s-era redbrick juvenile detention center on North River Street in downtown Wilkes-Barre was "an absolute dump and absolute disgrace," Ciavarella told reporters. He began lobbying for a new one.

In April of 2000 he approached Luzerne County's three commissioners about building a new detention center. "The place is old," he insisted in a public meeting. "It suffers from leaky pipes that we can't get to because they're buried behind two-foot thick concrete walls and the interior is infested with cockroaches and rodents."

State and county officials who had recently certified the place as safe didn't agree, while county commissioners worried about costs. Why not renovate the old building or turn a local nursing home into a new kid jail? They tabled Ciavarella's idea. Scooch, though, pressed on. If his scared-straight methods were to work, he would need a place to house all the kids he punished.

Four men together built two for-profit juvenile detention centers in northeastern Pennsylvania and then manipulated county government, the courts, children and youth, and taxpayer monies to enrich themselves. Clockwise from top left: former Juvenile Court Judge Mark Ciavarella; former President Judge Michael Conahan; developer Robert Mericle; and former personal injury lawyer Robert Powell.

FOUR MEN AND TWO BUILDINGS

If Judge Mark Ciavarella was brash and boastful, his closest courthouse friend, Judge Michael Conahan, was a model of reserve, like a poker player who kept his cards cemented to his chest. His quiet, though, belied immense power. Beefy, ruddy, with a thick neck, white hair, and a horizontal line for a mouth, Conahan was elected in 1994 and quickly rose to the top of the courthouse food chain, taking over as president judge, or the administrative head of the court, in 2002. He was also a businessman, with an array of investments from an ambulance service to a beer distributorship to a strip club, the Golden Slipper Lounge.

The two judges behaved differently on the bench. Ciavarella could be mocking and cruel, especially to children, while Conahan was polite in court and ruthless behind closed doors. Where Ciavarella grew up in a working-class neighborhood in Wilkes-Barre, Conahan came from relative privilege in nearby Hazleton, a Luzerne County town that sits on an anthracite mountain and features a colorful past—of corruption, firebombings, and murders of law enforcement officials, according to a 1977 series of stories in the *Philadelphia Inquirer*. It called Hazleton "Mob City."

Strange, violent things happened in Mob City, and all of it under a cloak of silence, the newspaper noted. "Nobody sees anything, nobody hears anything and nobody talks about anything," read one story, quoting a high-placed official.

Conahan's family ran a funeral parlor and his father, Joe, was a three-term mayor who was once caught awarding a government contract to a friend. Money, Joe Conahan conveyed to his eight children, equaled success. Conahan earned his law degree from Temple University, where some classmates described a low-key student who remained "under the radar."

Both Ciavarella and Conahan grew up with brutish fathers. Conahan "was beaten mercilessly" by his father when he was a teenager "for simply forgetting to stoke the family furnace at the funeral home," a lawyer defending Conahan later said. The assaultive parenting left psychological scars that Conahan later numbed with alcohol, clouding his judgment, his lawyer noted.

The two men grew to be "very, very close friends," Conahan told documentarians. They bought houses next to each other in upscale Mountain Top, south of Wilkes-Barre. They bought an

RV together, traveled with their wives together, invested in joint real estate ventures, and Conahan made personal zero-interest loans to his spendthrift friend.

In Ciavarella's view, Conahan was the perfect accomplice for a new kid jail. He straddled worlds—he knew business and government, and he was already running the courthouse, and the county, like his kingdom. The two men began to put their heads together with the idea of building a new, for-profit jail for kids, though they couldn't do it alone. They looked to old friends with money and influence, and Conahan soon tapped one from childhood.

His name was Robert Powell, and he had what the judges were looking for—assets and a will to invest them, along with close connections to county government. Powell was a former Division 1 college basketball player with slicked-back hair that receded into a dramatic widow's peak. He ran his own law firm, won millions as a personal injury lawyer, and enjoyed a lifestyle of conspicuous wealth.

Powell was also the chief lawyer for the local planning commission, which meant that he understood the rules, and knew the people in charge, when it came to buying and developing commercial property in the county. Newspapers said he flouted those rules. An editorial writer called Powell a "local man of mystery" after he failed to disclose his sources of income, as required by law, while on the county payroll.

Judge Ciavarella, meanwhile, reached out to his own childhood friend, another man with deep pockets and powerful connections. His name was Robert Mericle, and he was the biggest commercial real estate developer in northeastern Pennsylvania. Mericle's name graced hundreds of for-sale signs in rural parcels around the Wyoming Valley. He had benefited from many state-funded projects over the years and in turn gave generously to political campaigns, including Ciavarella's. Mericle had gifted Ciavarella with everything from Cabbage Patch Kid dolls from an early business venture to Broadway tickets to five thousand dollars in cash annually toward the judge's chosen vacation.

☍☍☍

In early 2001 the four men met: the two judges, lawyer Powell, and developer Mericle. They flushed out a plan. Powell would create a new juvenile detention center for the county to lock up law-breaking youth. It would operate for profit, and the government would provide that profit, by reimbursing Powell for every day that every youngster was jailed. The plan might've been fine had the government and the public known and agreed.

But the savvy quartet built their creation quietly, out of public view, combining their know-how and connections in finance, public projects, county land use, and development. Indeed, they speculated with confidence that the county would go along eventually.

Early on, all four men made sure their names didn't directly appear on the paperwork associated with the project. Robert Powell founded a new company, Pennsylvania Child Care. Who owned Pennsylvania Child Care? It was co-owned. Who were the co-owners? One was called Vision Holdings. What was Vision Holdings? An offshore investment company, with no named owner. A co-owner of Pennsylvania Child Care was a person with a name, of distinction: Gregory Zappala, an investment banker who was the son of a former state supreme court chief justice.

Powell's newly created Pennsylvania Child Care got a loan to buy land in an industrial park north of Wilkes-Barre, in Pittston Township. The kid prison would sit alongside trucking companies, warehouses, and a toilet tissue distributor. A residential neighborhood sat nearby.

In June of 2001, a cryptic zoning application landed with a township zoning officer. He reviewed a two-page write-up that described itself as a "facility for the Luzerne County Youth Center for pre-adjudicated juveniles."

The zoning officer, who was more familiar with building codes and sewer drainage than with which lands could be used for what purpose, thought he was looking at a youth rec center. It included a basketball court. He called a representative for the project who did not dissuade him from that view. "Luzerne County," the zoning officer reasoned, must've meant the building was for public use, which was permitted in the industrial zone. He missed the meaning of "pre-adjudicated juveniles" and signed off.

It was two years before local citizens learned a youth jail had materialized in their neighborhood. "Residents still can't believe a 48-bed juvenile detention center was signed, sealed and delivered to their own backyard without a chance for them to air their gripes and concerns," read the newspaper story in the *Times Leader*. "No public hearings. No public notices of the proposed project. No chance to round up signatures for petitions or write letters opposing the center."

‍‌‌‌‌ ⛓

After the approval, Powell needed more money to build the building, a greater challenge. Why would any bank offer a loan to Powell? With what source of income would Pennsylvania Child Care repay the loan? It sounded risky.

Judge Conahan found a way. In January of 2002, the month he became the president judge of the county court system, Conahan drafted a document. He called it a "placement guarantee agreement." It promised that Luzerne County would send its child criminals to the detention-center-to-be. He wrote that the county would pay Pennsylvania Child Care about $1.3 million a year to operate the youth jail. The county's obligation to pay was "absolute and unconditional," Conahan wrote. He signed the document and handed it off to Powell.

The president judge had no authority to create the document. Only the county commissioners were able to oversee such decisions. But Conahan did it anyway. And it worked: Powell got his financing.

Mericle, who was the lowest bidder and won the project, soon broke ground. One day he paid a visit to Ciavarella in his chambers. "This is your lucky day," he told the judge. Mericle was offering a finder's fee of 10 percent of the cost of the project, or about $1 million.

"Is this legal? Is this something you can do?" the judge later recalled asking.

"I do it all the time," Mericle said. "Anybody that brings me a project, I pay them a finder's fee, and I'm gonna pay you one."

As astonished as a lottery winner, Ciavarella rushed to Judge Conahan's chambers to share the news and split the money. Conahan had put the deal together, Ciavarella reasoned, so Conahan deserved half. Joyful, Conahan threw his pencil in the air and told Ciavarella he was lucky to know Mericle. "That's one hell of a friend," he said.

The county, though, was still sending youths to the old North River Street center, so Ciavarella stepped up his public worry over the hazards of the old lockup—though his financial gain with the new one would later undercut his sincerity: "I don't need to go to bed at night worrying if some children have the ceiling falling down on them or that they were bit by a rodent," he told a reporter in 2002. "It's not fair to me and it's not fair to the kids."

Conahan made way for the detention center under construction by not sending children, staff, or money to the old one. In October of 2002 he ordered the probation department to stop sending children to North River Street. In December he stripped funding for the following year from the old center's staff of sixteen. The same month he returned the center's license to the state office that had just renewed it. Only county commissioners had the legal authority to shut down the county detention facility, but once again Conahan took that action on his own, without county approval. But no one at the time objected.

In January of 2003 Conahan and Ciavarella began receiving their $1 million from Mericle in a twisty series of wires and transfers meant to hide the money. A February 6 ribbon cutting at Pennsylvania Child Care made it real. Now all the owners needed was a steady stream of juvenile delinquents to fill the beds.

---◦◦◦◦◦◦◦--- CHAPTER 5 ---◦◦◦◦◦◦◦---

KIDS FOR CASH

◦◦◦◦◦◦◦◦◦◦◦◦◦◦◦◦◦◦◦◦◦◦◦◦◦◦◦◦◦◦

In early 2003, Judge Mark Ciavarella had more reason than ever to lock up children, no matter how ordinary their sins. In addition to peddling his zero-tolerance philosophy, he had lobbied publicly and with gusto for the all-new detention center. His friends had bought the land, finagled the loans, built the building, and rewarded him and President Judge Michael Conahan with $1 million. Now the owners of the new kid lockup had bills to manage and a profit to turn. Like other for-profit detention centers, the new Pennsylvania Child Care relied on head counts to make money. They needed a steady stream of misbehaving kids to keep the place full. The key job of admissions fell to Ciavarella.

The old, decrepit North River Street center held twenty-two beds and was, before Ciavarella, half-empty. The new lockup had forty-eight metal beds bolted to the floor, and the entrepreneurial owners would add another cellblock for a total of sixty beds. Then two years later, owners Robert Powell and Gregory Zappala decided to build yet another detention center. Other counties from around the state could send their delinquents to either lockup, they reasoned. With the same builder, Robert Mericle, they built a second, even larger facility in Butler County and called it Western Pennsylvania Child Care. This sister detention center had ninety-nine beds. The addition to the first and the creation of the second led to another $1.15 million gift from Mericle to the judges, bringing the total in "finder's fees," later referred to in criminal court as "kickbacks," to $2.15 million. But where, now, would Ciavarella, as chief supplier, find enough children and youth to fill all those beds? That was his challenge.

◖◖◖

With the help of his close friend President Judge Michael Conahan, Ciavarella began bending and twisting the county juvenile system to his will—enlarging the pool of inmates, expanding his definition of "delinquent," and finding myriad ways to turn kids into cash. As early as late 2002, just before the youth jail opened, Ciavarella assembled the county probation staff and applied ramrod pressure. "I want PA [Pennsylvania] Child Care filled at all times," Ciavarella told them, "and I don't care if we have to bankrupt the county to do it. Is that clear?"

Three days after Pennsylvania Child Care opened, Ciavarella issued another command to widen his dragnet: all youths who violated their probation were to be locked up, no matter how incidental the violation—missed curfew, a failed marijuana test, or tardiness to court-ordered community service or counseling. And once in lockup, a child's stay could lengthen interminably, becoming a virtual ringing cash register as the days accrued. Ciavarella often ordered psychological evaluations, which might mean weeks of waiting for the appointment with the court psychologist. That psychologist happened to be a Conahan relative, later outed by the state for overcharging and submitting reports that were comprised of the same boilerplate language, cut and pasted over and over again. One report even contained the wrong name of the youth being evaluated.

Ciavarella's judicial methods had, from the start of his tenure, led to a steady rise in the number of county youths sent away from home. Still, the year the new detention center opened smashed records. He had taken over juvenile court in the fall of 1996, a year when sixty youths from Luzerne County were sent to detention. By the end of 2003, the year Pennsylvania Child Care opened, Ciavarella had sent 330 youths to detention, more than double the state rate and the highest placement rate of any county in the state. Tiny Luzerne County comprised less than 3 percent of the state's population in 2003—but was responsible for 22 percent of juvenile placements.

The explosion in juvenile detainees translated into quick dollars for the kid prison owners and their friends. Most business start-ups take two to three years to become profitable. Pennsylvania Child Care cleared a $1 million profit in its first year of operation. And that number would grow.

And grow. Placing a child in the juvenile justice system is like pulling them into quicksand, experts say. Once lodged in the unyielding muck of that system, youths may have great difficulty getting out. And Ciavarella, with his strict edicts, helped them sink in ever-deeper. Youths detained, once released, were placed on probation. Those on probation, with Ciavarella's trip wires, were easily caught violating probation. The violation required a return to detention. Release from detention meant a return to probation, starting the cycle again.

And that was true in Luzerne County even if the original offense was unfounded.

David W. was fourteen when called to Ciavarella's courtroom as a witness for a friend accused of assault. Soon Judge Ciavarella ordered the bailiff to shackle David W. and sentenced him to seventy days in detention. "Who takes a kid who didn't do anything away from their parents?" David W. later wondered. "Some guy showed up and said I kicked a kid while he was on the ground. I wasn't able to say a word. I didn't touch anybody. I was put in shackles."

Once released, David W. was placed on probation. One day after school at a friend's house he realized he was late for his 7:00 p.m. home curfew. His friend rushed him home but drove so fast he crashed the car. David W. broke his femur, was hospitalized, and got hooked on pain medications. Today he is clean and sober and works as a pipeline welder. But he says the false conviction changed the course of his life. "I'm thirty-three years old and still have trouble seventeen years later," he later said under oath.

President Judge Conahan helped to impart to the courthouse staff, in a gruff manner, the urgent need to imprison kids. In one example, state guidelines required new juvenile detention centers to conduct soft openings, as with a new business. The state refused reimbursements to the county unless it followed guidelines to go slow filling beds once the doors of Pennsylvania Child Care opened. The judges balked. In late February of 2003 Ciavarella called into his office Sandra Brulo, the chief of Luzerne County juvenile probation, and handed her the phone. It was "the boss."

"Judge Conahan began screaming at me and accused me of being responsible for the ramping up limits," Brulo later wrote to a state committee. "He said Robert Powell had bills to pay," and the limits were hurting admissions.

Brulo pressed her staff to lock up more kids.

"Who?" a placement officer asked.

"Just fill the beds," she snapped.

The placement officer rounded up some county youths from outlying juvenile facilities. At least that way they'd be close to home.

Ciavarella, too, lassoed more kids—by sending ordinary young people to detention for preposterous violations like jaywalking, swearing, or underage drinking. He detained young teens for yelling at a parent or hurling a sandal, a pillow, or, as in one case, a piece of steak during shouting matches. He turned ordinary objects, in children's hands, into weapons: a pencil sharpener was a "weapon" on school grounds, rock-throwing a "propulsion of missiles," and a lice bomb a "weapon of mass destruction." A girl was jailed for giving her middle finger to a police officer, a gesture that is protected under a citizen's first amendment right to freedom of speech.

His punishments rarely fit the so-called crimes. In 2004, at age sixteen, Rebecca Hackney was stopped by a policer officer for driving the wrong way down a one-way street without her driver's license. Ciavarella judged her delinquent. Then he made a bizarre comment, Hackney later said under oath: "I want you to count the number of buttons on your blouse, and that's the number of months . . . that you're going away for."

Hackney laughed. She thought the judge was joking. She counted the buttons. There were eleven. Ciavarella sentenced her to eleven months of detention.

GCO

Ciavarella also vacuumed up cash through "fines court," which was not unlike the debtors' prisons in the US, banned in 1833, or those in England dramatized in the best-selling novels by Charles Dickens. In Luzerne County in the 2000s, it was not the adult debtors but the debtors' children who were locked up. Under Pennsylvania law at the time, a child judged delinquent was placed under the custody of the court. Parents lost custody of their child and were then billed for child support and court fees. In short, Ciavarella imprisoned youngsters illegally, then charged their parents for the state's cost of their child's imprisonment. If parents were unable to pay, the county could take them to court—and hold their child in detention or on probation until the family paid up. The monies went into a fund later said to be aimed at probation department expenses. But the county, it was later found, had no knowledge of this money, what was referred to in hearings as a slush fund to be used at the judge's discretion. "It was just a horrible situation," said one Philadelphia lawyer and child advocate who later helped to expose the fines court practice.

Ciavarella presided over fines court beginning as early as 1999, operating at best like a collections agent, at worst a kidnapper. One transcript from September of 2001 showed eighty-two youths and their families had been summoned to a single day of fines court for lack of payment. Another, from 2004, recorded Ciavarella's interrogation of a small boy, Ryan, who stood before him with his mother. "How old are you?" Ciavarella asked.

"Eleven," said Ryan, who stood four-foot-two and weighed sixty-three pounds.

"There was a fine imposed," Ciavarella said. "You didn't pay it. Disorderly conduct . . . So you didn't pay that one. Do you have $488.50?"

The boy shook his head that he did not.

"Very good," Ciavarella said. "He's remanded. He can stay [imprisoned] until he pays the fines."

The boy's mother cut in. "It's actually more than that," she said. "I got something [else] in the mail. I received [a notice] in the mail that he owed $850 for something. I think it was due by the 15th of January."

The higher fine, she said, would also soon be overdue.

"We'll get that," Ciavarella assured her. "By the time he gets out he'll be able to go back for the next one."

He looked at the boy. "You're having a great day."

To the court staff: "Put the cuffs on him and get him out of [here]."

When one sixteen-year-old teen said he lacked the more than four-hundred-dollar fine assessed for smoking in school, his mother told Ciavarella she would cover the cost. The judge snapped at mother and son, insisting the youth pay his own fine.

He turned to the teen. "Your mommy can't help you now."

He sent the boy away.

The fees and fines followed kids home as families struggled to pay. After Carisa Tomkiel, the street-sign scribbler, was released from detention, she was sentenced to house arrest. The eighth grader was confined to her family's West Pittston home with a 24-7 ankle monitor, unable to attend school. The Tomkiels were charged for the parole officer visit to install the monitoring, for

The Tomkiel family kept receipts from fees paid to the court for their daughter's incarceration and lengthy term of probation. Court fines and fees levied against families of jailed children, as well as the costs of treatment for the traumatic effects of incarceration afterward, added up to tens of thousands of dollars in some cases, leading to lost homes and drained retirement savings.

the ankle monitor itself, and for the device in their home that notified probation if Carisa stepped onto her front porch or spent too much time on the phone. Between the lawyer fees, the court costs, restitution, and six months of probation, the Tomkiels paid roughly five thousand dollars in all for their daughter's detention. Andrea Tomkiel worked part time at a doughnut shop and her husband managed a garage. The monthly notices from the court were like collections billing. Every month the Tomkiels paid thirty-five dollars toward the fees, and every month the total they owed remained the same, at $570, or crept higher. Upon Carisa's release from probation six months later, they still owed the court, but those costs were a trifle compared with their daughter's deteriorating morale.

⊖⊖⊖

And that was the thing. The court's drive to fill beds and fleece people didn't just flatten bank accounts. The monetizing of juvenile justice destroyed children's mental health. Under Ciavarella, the most emotionally fragile children and families who entered his courtroom sustained some of the greatest costs.

⊖⊖⊖

Before Kelcy Morgans's appearance in 2005, her father penned a beseeching letter to the "Good Judge" Ciavarella, imploring him to have mercy on his daughter. At fifteen, she was at a "tipping point." She had suffered tragic events in early childhood but was regaining her footing. She was committed enough to her progress that she had reported her own misstep to her probation officer: smoking two puffs of a marijuana cigarette. A test had confirmed trace amounts. Kelcy had made some irrational decisions in the past, in part due to mental health issues documented by doctors, her father wrote.

"But I'm starting to see some of the traits of the little girl I love so much slowly return," he added. "This is a very fragile situation for all of us. Any more strife could set her back when we want so desperately to see her inch forward. Please don't douse this flickering flame; It may never be able to be re-ignited."

But in the courtroom, Ciavarella ordered Kelcy to count birds on the windowsill. "How many pigeons do you see outside that window?" Ciavarella asked.

"Six?" she asked.

"That's right. You are going away for six months!"

The judge asked Kelcy if she had anything to say for herself.

"Yes," she said, "I would like to say something."

"You say *one word* and I'll put you away for another ninety

Traumatic events from childhood had left Kelcy Morgans in a fragile though improving state when she told her probation officer that she had smoked two puffs of a marijuana cigarette. Her father, Robert Morgans, penned a letter to the juvenile judge to plead for mercy in sentencing Kelcy. "Any more strife could set her back," he wrote, "when we so desperately want to see her inch forward. Please don't douse this flickering flame."

Good Judge :

My daughter Kelcy is a good kid basically. This past year has been a tough one for her and her family.

Besides the normal teenage dificulties most kids her age have, she has physical and mental issues compounding her life.

These problems are duly documented by the Medical Community.

This is not an excuse for her behavior; it's a fact

We and she know she has had made some irrational decisions affected by her conditions, but I'm starting to see some of the traits of the little girl I love so much slowly return

This is a very fragile situation for all of us.

any more strife could set her back when we need so desperately to see her inch forward.

Please don't douse this flickering flame; it may never be able to be re-ignited.

As a father I pray for your leniency.

God Bless this family. Thank you

Sincerly : Robert U. Morgans

days," Ciavarella blasted, in his great-and-powerful voice, as the Morganses recalled.

He turned to a court worker. "Cuff her! Get her out of my courtroom!"

Her probation officer had assured the Morganses that Kelcy would go home. But now the worker cried as she knelt before Kelcy with a set of cuffs and leg irons. "I'm so sorry, I don't know what's going on," the worker repeated over and over.

"None of us had any idea," reflected Kelcy, today a struggling mother of four. "We just knew something was wrong. 'Why?' we wondered. We blamed ourselves. That's the battle. You know right from wrong but then you go through this and you're constantly at war with your own instincts. Was *I* wrong or were *they* wrong? It's like a movie that constantly plays in your head. When is it gonna stop or will it ever?"

CHAPTER 6

KINGDOM OF SILENCE

The freakish treatment of children, the senseless filling of detention centers, and the scheming existence of fines court continued year after year throughout the 2000s in part due to the skills of an overlord, President Judge Michael Conahan. He ruled from the magisterial Luzerne County Courthouse, a neoclassical gem built a century ago on the banks of the Susquehanna. The stately building, listed in the historic registry, features marble staircases and mahogany trim, intricate stained glass and sprawling murals, and a one-hundred-foot-tall ceiling dome—all creating a postcard setting fit for a wedding ceremony, which, in fact, the county

During a period in the late 2000s the courthouse earned a nickname, the Plunder Dome, and court watchers said President Judge Michael Conahan treated it like his kingdom. Witnesses later testified to delivering envelopes of cash to Conahan's office, though the ex-judge was never convicted of taking bribes or case fixing.

offers at a cost of five hundred dollars. A scroll in a courthouse mural is inscribed with a Latin phrase that translates as: "Though the heavens may fall, justice must prevail."

While Judge Mark Ciavarella administered his brand of justice from the drab-looking courthouse annex across town, President Judge Conahan ruled all of the county courts from his more kingly chambers on the river. From there Conahan manipulated people and the law, creating a forcefield of fear, silence, and complicity that helped to protect his lucrative schemes.

Operating like a Mafia boss, and regularly consorting with one, Conahan was a study in leveraging power. He ran the courthouse by first collecting favors, then requiring them in return. He sought indebtedness compulsively—by offering jobs, loans, or other breaks to people who then owed him. He stripped hiring powers from department heads and gave them to himself, then appointed and protected allies and decimated enemies. His power was for sale, and he accepted cash bribes throughout his tenure, court witnesses later testified. His influence "extended to reach nearly everything that happened under the domes of the Luzerne County Courthouse," said one county judge at the time. The courts ran the county, a former commissioner said, not the other way around. An editorial writer nicknamed the courthouse under Conahan the Plunder Dome.

Conahan filled his Plunder Dome with family and friends. There were rules against nepotism, or the practice of just such hiring, but Conahan hired straight from his address book and extended family dinner table, making the payroll look like a family tree. Conahan's brother-in-law, Frank Vita, was appointed the juvenile court's psychologist without any hiring contract or approval from the county. Vita overcharged for his services and exaggerated his hours of work, auditors later said. Conahan's first cousin, William Sharkey, the court administrator, handled courthouse money and was later convicted of stealing a lot of it. Sharkey's girlfriend, son, and daughter all held positions in county probation. Another daughter was granted an internship.

Conahan's nephew was a probation officer. A second Conahan brother-in-law became "jury management supervisor." Conahan created a tier of court employees, or tipstaff, under his control with unidentified job descriptions. In early 2004, when an election defeat caused an administrative turnover of county staff, Conahan created nine new jobs for the newly jobless in the courthouse, some with higher salaries than before, reporters wrote.

The joke was that if you worked in the Hazleton office and

needed a kidney transplant, "you did not have to go far" since most employees were related by blood, said the former juvenile probation chief, Sandra Brulo, under oath.

Ciavarella, too, surrounded himself with friends and family. His daughter was an assistant district attorney. The county payroll also included Ciavarella's former neighbor, his daughter's boyfriend and former boyfriend, his wife's nephew and his wife's nephew's wife, a daughter of Ciavarella family friends, and a Ciavarella cousin.

All owed some or all of the food on their tables to the judges, creating a scrim of fear and intimidation reminiscent of the days of rogue coal operators and Mafia criminality.

❦❦❦

The scared loyalists watched, silently, as the judges' enemies were punished with dramatic demotions, arrests for contempt of court, poor outcomes in court cases, or frivolous lawsuits. Word got around the courthouse fast. The two judges even controlled elections, in part by bullying the local bar association, whose three-hundred-odd lawyers felt obligated to donate to the judges' campaigns or else. When a critic, Steve Flood, the county controller, showed open suspicion of some of the judges' actions, his reelection was doomed. Samuel Stretton, the controller's solicitor and a personal friend, was in Flood's office one day in 2005 when a fellow lawyer called to apologize for his lack of support for Flood's reelection. "Steve, we would like to contribute to you, but we were told by Conahan, 'You'll never win a case in the county' if we do," Stretton later told authorities under oath. Flood lost the primary.

Another facet of Conahan's intimidating power had to do with his close connection to organized crime. When not in his chambers or on the bench, Conahan talked over court business in the back booth of Perkins, the chain pancake house situated on a county road sprawling with budget motels and eateries not far from downtown Wilkes-Barre.

There Conahan met as often as three times a week with a close and longtime friend, William "Big Billy" D'Elia, a tall, silver-haired man known to the federal government as one of the most active and powerful Mafia bosses in the country. D'Elia had been the protégée, driver, and personal bodyguard of Russell Bufalino, the longtime leader of the Bufalino crime family of northeastern Pennsylvania, even as organized crime ebbed in the twenty-first century. D'Elia and Bufalino had been like father and son, and when Bufalino died in 1994, D'Elia took over the Bufalino operations. Books and a movie had speculated that Bufalino ordered the killing of Jimmy Hoffa, the Detroit labor union leader who vanished in 1975. That disappearance has never been explained. But decades later, the government was still keeping close track of D'Elia.

The feds watched D'Elia wherever he went. In 2006 they charged him with laundering drug money, which meant passing money made by selling drugs through a series of accounts in order to hide the illegally earned sums. As the case proceeded, the federal government also charged D'Elia with trying to have a witness in the case against him murdered. He would eventually plead guilty to money laundering and witness tampering and serve time in prison. But up until a month before going to prison, he had breakfast with Conahan.

At Perkins, the men met early in the morning and ordered ham-and-cheese omelets, two waitresses later testified. Then, with files and paperwork spread out next to packets of jellies, syrups, and sweeteners, the two men studied and talked about court cases. Sometimes they were joined by a third man, who would eventually testify against them. The third man later said Conahan and D'Elia were "fixing" court cases. Instead of an impartial judge or jury hearing a case and deciding its outcome on the basis of evidence and witness testimony, the judge and the mob boss just decided upon guilt or innocence over breakfast, frequently leading D'Elia to pay cash to Conahan for a particular outcome, witnesses later testified. One courthouse guard said under oath that she delivered envelopes directly from D'Elia's car in the parking lot to Conahan's chambers. But neither the judge nor the mob boss has ever been convicted of case fixing.

At one point Ciavarella expressed worry to Conahan about those Perkins meetings. Was it a good idea for the president judge to be seen in public with a known mob boss? Conahan shrugged it off. D'Elia had been a friend for so long—thirty years—it would arouse no suspicion, he said.

But Ciavarella was right. Federal agents were keeping track of D'Elia. It was their job to root out organized crime. If D'Elia was still operating illegal businesses and conspiring with others in those ventures, who were his friends? Agents followed him to Perkins. They surveilled him on those early morning visits. Who was D'Elia meeting with so often, they wondered? And why?

Soon the agents' question changed. Why was a Mafia boss meeting three times a week with the president judge of the county?

CHAPTER 7

DIVERGENCE

By 2003, the judges had upgraded to noticeably flashier lifestyles while Robert Powell, the detention-center owner, splurged on ever more extravagant displays of luxury. All three men appeared to have come into sudden wealth.

The year beds began filling at Pennsylvania Child Care, a new company sprung up in Florida. Pinnacle Group of Jupiter was managed by the judges' wives, Barbara Conahan and Cindy Ciavarella. As more and more children and youth were sent to juvenile detention, millions in taxpayer dollars intended for their care detoured in one form or another to Pinnacle in Florida. Pinnacle in turn spent the money.

In 2004 the judges, through their new company, Pinnacle, bought themselves a newly constructed luxury condominium in

Jupiter, a beach town for the wealthy in northern Palm Beach County. The three-bedroom, three-bath, 2,600-square-foot vacation residence perched above the Intracoastal Waterway, and the resort-like complex sparkled with the status markers of the rich: luxury cars, shooting fountains, giant palms, a putting green. Today it features a tiered movie theater with plush recliners, a five-star French restaurant, a sushi bar, and an art gallery.

The balcony of the unfinished third-floor condo overlooked the Jupiter Yacht Club, where fishing, sailing, and cruising vessels bobbed in their slips. One was called *Reel Justice*, and it belonged to Robert Powell, who in 2002 bought the fifty-six-foot fishing yacht for $1.3 million. The vessel included a $6,820 teak fishing chair, and Powell hired a captain to take friends and family on ocean fishing jaunts. When docked, the yacht drew noisy revelers—until the yacht club tried suing Powell to terminate his boat slip sublease. The *Reel Justice* eventually found another home.

GƎO

Back in Pennsylvania, detained children and youth were living in more sober and austere settings—sleeping in pup tents in the snow of a wilderness camp, or sleeping on cafeteria floors in a detention center, or not sleeping at all to watch for middle-of-the-night attacks by other youths or staff at a notorious reform school. They dined on jailhouse food, like Styrofoam cups of ramen noodles served in lukewarm water. "People would put the seasoning pack in the warm water and drink that, then eat the dry, hard ramen," reported one detained youth.

Pennsylvania law says juvenile detention should be a place of last resort for "supervision, care and rehabilitation" to help children become successful adults. Courts should separate a child from

The year before the opening of his for-profit juvenile detention center, Robert Powell bought a 56-foot fishing yacht, the *Reel Justice*, for $1.3 million. He kept the vessel at the Jupiter Yacht Club in Florida for a time. The yacht included a $6,820 teak fishing chair, and Powell hired a captain to take friends and family on fishing jaunts.

their family "only when necessary," using the "least restrictive intervention" for the "minimum amount of time." That's because of the well-documented harm caused by incarcerating children.

Ciavarella flouted those guidelines. Some beds at Pennsylvania Child Care were supposed to be for treatment, offering services on a long-term basis to children with some underlying issues, if the court so ordered. But for youths awaiting their first court hearing, state guidelines required that they be locked up only if a danger to themselves or others. All other youths should have remained at home with their families until their day in court. But the judge locked up kids who were no danger to anyone, and then inexplicably shuffled them, in shackles, to other centers around the state, sometimes rousing them in the middle of the night to be transported elsewhere.

At sentencing, Ciavarella placed youths in facilities ranging from mental health centers to wilderness programs, military-style boot camps, reform schools, or higher-security youth prisons in other states, including New Jersey, Ohio, and Utah.

⟳

Wherever the children landed, so began their entry into the harrowing culture of youth incarceration. Luzerne kids, jailed most frequently for first-time and trivial offenses, were dropped into locked institutions alongside more sophisticated youths— usually older teens convicted of assaulting a police officer, or killing a parent, or committing armed robbery, or stealing a car. "And then there were people from Luzerne County," said one formerly detained youth, now an adult, in sworn testimony, "that were in there for stealing a pack of M & Ms or getting in a tiff with their high school teacher."

The armed robbers and drug dealers often laughed at the petty crimes of the Luzerne youth. But the older inmates assumed the role of teachers. The sophisticates taught the newbies how to make explosives, or rob a store, or sell drugs without getting caught. "I learned how to become a criminal when I was supposed to learn to go to prom, you know, get my driver's license," one Luzerne County youth said under oath. "[Those] were the best years . . . supposed to be, of my life, and instead I'm learning how to sharpen a toothbrush [into a knife]."

A third young man, ten when sentenced, said he was essentially brainwashed by the older boys who took him under their wing. Homework, school, college, and graduation were a waste of time, they advised. A real job was meaningless. "You'll be a cog in a machine and then drop dead," the older youths told him, the young man testified. "You're better off selling drugs."

Added a woman detained at fifteen: "I didn't know anything about drugs [before] and I came out with a PhD."

⌗

As detained kids from Luzerne County aligned themselves with more hardened criminals, the judges and Powell kept adding to their net worth and collection of expensive toys. In 2005, the year that his second detention center, Western Pennsylvania Child Care, opened, Robert Powell spent $2.6 million on a corporate turbo jet. The plane's interior included buckskin leather seats, a couch, gold-plated fixtures, and a state-of-the-art sound system. The cost of flying the jet came to about $2,158 an hour. Auditors later said the plane cost Powell about $1 million a year to operate, much of the monies swiped from detention center earnings.

State auditors later flagged other expenses: a $4,500 chartered fishing trip, and $5,800 in limousine services to college basketball games and shopping, and $3,500 for a custom men's suit from a New York City tailor, and membership in a Philadelphia dining club, and Pittsburgh Steelers football tickets, and golf outings that included promotional towels and T-shirts, umbrellas, visors, and pens, all expensed to detention center and related accounts.

The same state audit questioned $1 million in consulting fees—to other companies owned by Robert Powell. Meanwhile the auditors later said the county paid the detention centers more than $140,000 for beds that remained empty.

⌗

And meanwhile, the youths Ciavarella locked up were enduring beatings, sexual assaults, verbal abuse, and lengths of stay that far outstripped their supposed misdeeds. The catalog of harms done fill spreadsheets in later civil court actions and transcripts from victim testimony. Those harms range from broken limbs to untreated infections, mental health breakdowns, deaths from drug overdoses, and suicide. Even minor injuries had consequences.

April Jerock acquired a toenail infection after going barefoot in the communal showers at Pennsylvania Child Care. No one had told her to wear flip-flops. "It's so silly," she said years later. "But it haunts me like the day is long. I have gone through medications, tried the strong stuff, the not-so-strong stuff. It's my little relic, I guess."

Angelia, Carisa Tomkiel's best friend, was sent directly from Ciavarella's courtroom to a wilderness camp despite her epilepsy. She was soon deemed too medically fragile to stay and transferred to a detention center closer to home. Two days later Angelia, in the throes of a seizure, banged her head against a brick wall and broke her braces. Her mother learned of the seizure from an acquaintance who worked at the center and tipped her off, she later said under oath.

And while assaults left physical and emotional scars, most youths had their schooling interrupted or aborted, leading to a lifetime shadowed by poverty. One man said under oath that his schooling in detention consisted of watching *The Magic School Bus*, the animated TV series. A woman said hers amounted to word searches and crossword puzzles. Jessica Van Reeth said under oath that while detained she was taught by uncertified teachers acting like babysitters: a man who exercised at a gym taught health; an undergraduate in pre-K education taught English. Math class consisted of two worksheets per week without instruction.

The deplorable schooling stymied kids upon coming home. Once Elizabeth Habel, a straight-A student when first detained, returned home, she was dropped into the eleventh grade. She had been doing multiplication worksheets in detention, which had not prepared her for algebra. When a classmate hurled a pencil at her, she reacted with the one skill she had been taught in detention: survival. "I got up as the teacher was teaching and I walked over to [the classmate's] desk and I threw all his books on the floor and I threw the pencil in his face and said, 'Don't ever throw your pencil at my face again.'"

The school district sent her to the alternative learning school and three months later the young, geeky girl, the straight-A student, her father's "little brain," dropped out of high school.

∞

As time wore on, Robert Powell's big spending was hidden by his fancy accounting, auditors said. He moved money around like peas in a shell game, making a series of interest-free loans from Pennsylvania Child Care to a web of companies he owned, essentially loaning money from himself to himself for free. Hundreds of thousands of dollars meant for Pennsylvania Child Care were funneled by Powell to his law firm and to his other companies, the government later found.

The transactions, unsurprisingly, starved the detention centers. Pennsylvania Child Care began receiving utility shutoff notices. To keep the place running, Powell took out new, high-interest loans, paying more than $51,000 in interest on one loan alone. He was paying money to borrow money because he had used up the money intended for detained children on himself and his associates.

And children and youth, meanwhile, began to manifest

psychological and social harms more difficult to see or fix than a broken bone on an X-ray. Kids returned home altered—more reclusive or combative, more troubled or hopeless, less successful in school. And the trauma of detention dragged them down as they grew up, each stage a struggle, magnified. "So, so many of these kids were just so, so traumatized," said Marie J. Yeager, an advocate for the Juvenile Law Center of Philadelphia. "If they didn't have problems going in, they certainly did coming out."

An attorney and national advocate for juvenile justice later compared the lush lifestyles of the moneymakers to the profound harms to children. "I've never encountered and I don't think that we will in our lifetimes, a case where literally thousands of kids' lives were just tossed aside in order for a couple of judges to make some money."

And later a sharp-tongued columnist, Mark Guydish, wrote that at the Luzerne County Courthouse, "Shameless" Ciavarella and "Cocky" Conahan together "gave justice a price tag, used their black robes to hide their own black hearts, and spent the profits partying in a luxury Florida condo like some brat heirs of the superrich."

However high flying, though, the conspirators soon learned that greed and self-interest can come between friends.

CHAPTER 8

VILLAIN OR VICTIM

On Christmas Eve of 2001 Robert Powell and his friend Michael Conahan had taken a drive to the rough site of their planned detention center. The two men smoked cigars while Powell described his grand vision. "You know," Conahan said to Powell, according to Powell's later testimony, "when we get all this done we're going to have to do something to take care of [Judge] Mark [Ciavarella]."

Two years later, and three days after the detention-center ribbon cutting in January of 2003, the promised $1 million payoff from builder Robert Mericle began its crooked path to the judges' pockets. The money's twists and turns later looked like a complex dot-to-dot sketch as the dollars traveled from builder Robert Mericle's real-estate company to Powell's law firm to a friend's bank account to a Conahan company and finally to the Pinnacle account in Florida, the one principally owned by the judges' wives. IRS and FBI investigators later tracked each leg of that winding path. When reporters from the *Times Leader* began to investigate, they tacked a series of poster-size white paper to a wall, placed photographs of the four men at four corners, made lists of their business holdings, and drew lines between men, money, and institutions to keep it all straight.

But no sooner had the money reached Ciavarella's wallet than he spent it to lift himself out of enormous debt. He was a boundless spender.

"He blew through hundreds of thousands of dollars," said Michael Consiglio, an assistant federal prosecutor. Ciavarella and Conahan had together bought a new Winnebago, which they used to drive with their wives on weekend trips to Penn State football games and NASCAR races. "It was like, 'I'm entitled to this; I see other people spending like this; I work hard. I don't care if I fall into debt, even if I'm underwater.' It was shortsighted and thoughtless."

ⴲ

And it left Ciavarella wanting more, Powell soon learned. In the fall of 2003, Powell was summoned to Ciavarella's chambers to meet with both judges. In addition to the payoff from builder Mericle, the judges now wanted cash directly from Powell. Wait, Powell said to the judges. "Don't tell me you blew through a million bucks already?" he asked, according to later court testimony. "Heh, heh, yeah, we burned through it," they replied.

Judge Ciavarella argued that it was only fair. He had been keeping close track of detention center admissions, since he was the unofficial admissions officer. Based on those numbers, he had been calculating Powell's profits on paper. He was able to wave the figures in front of Powell and insist on a cut. "You've been very successful up there," Ciavarella asserted bluntly. "I want in on it."

Powell started reaching into detention center funds to pay off the judges, agreeing to cover up the purpose of those payments in case anyone inquired. He began writing personal checks to Pinnacle in Florida with a notation in the memo line, "Rent," as if he were now a paying tenant at the Jupiter condo, paying fifteen thousand dollars a month to reside there. Investigators later poked holes in that story by noting that Powell began paying before the condo had walls or furnishings. He also set foot in the condo only once or twice. Powell wrote other checks with other notations having to do with "nautical fees" to keep his yacht docked at the yacht club. In fact, all of the checks were payoffs to the judges to keep Powell's detention centers full, Powell later testified.

Throughout 2004 Powell wrote seven checks totaling nearly $600,000. He thought that was plenty.

But the judges wanted more. And like most everyone else, Powell feared the black-robed duo. Sure, Powell was a bear of a man—six-foot-five and nearly 260 pounds—but he later said he could've been seven feet tall and named "Shaq," like the legendary basketball player, and still been unable to withstand the judges' bullying.

They had a firm grip on many aspects of his livelihood, he later said under oath. Without Ciavarella's constant flow of kids and the government's millions in reimbursements, he'd be unable to pay off the $12 million mortgage on Pennsylvania Child Care and the entire enterprise would fail, he feared. After all, Conahan had magically axed the old county detention center without any authority. He could do the same to Pennsylvania Child Care in an instant.

And Powell had a thriving, lucrative law practice. The judges had been more than friendly overseeing his multimillion-dollar awards. They could just as easily ruin him now—by ruling against him in his personal injury cases. He was dealing with the "two most powerful men in Luzerne County, they ran the show," he later said under oath. "They knew politicians and they knew mobsters and they flaunted their position with both of them."

Powell grew more nervous as his payments increased. He had helped to create a grand scheme and benefited. But now *he* felt like a victim—of extortion. "The lion was out of the cage and I was the bait," Powell said. The two judges were using their power to destroy him financially, extracting more and more money. "They were absolutely relentless," Powell said.

In 2005 Powell set off for Costa Rica to escape the judges' greedy demands. When he returned in June of 2006, he had resolved to quit the payoffs. At a meeting at Conahan's home he told both judges: "I'm not doing this anymore. I can't do this. This is not going to end well," he later said under oath.

After that the judges said they wanted all future payments in cash.

Powell left the country again in the summer of 2006, this time taking his family on a month-long vacation to Italy to evade the judges' demands. But a few days after his return the judges were calling like collection agents. "If you can take your children and your family to Italy," Ciavarella told Powell, "you can pay us."

Powell, increasingly flustered, began cashing checks and stuffing large bills into envelopes and FedEx boxes. His law partner delivered the boxes to Conahan via the back door of the courthouse, later saying she didn't know what was inside the boxes until one day in December of 2006, when she walked in on Powell in the private washroom of his law office, jamming bundled bunches of large bills into a box while cursing and muttering.

"These greedy [expletives] won't let me go," Powell said to his then-partner, Jill Moran, in one scene she later described under oath. He was clutching bundles of one-hundred-dollar and fifty-dollar bills.

"This is the last one," he muttered. "If anybody asks, this is the last one."

He added, "Take this to them, and hopefully it will be over."

By then the judges' accounts bulged with cash. Between Powell's gifts and Mericle's payments, the money-hungry jurists had secretly made about $2.8 million above and beyond their roughly $150,000 state salaries—in contrast to the youths and families at the bottom, the ones who had few resources to defend themselves in court, and who lost thousands in paying off the fees and fines when their children were locked up.

But whatever Powell's misgivings, he kept paying. Whatever others saw or felt in the juvenile courtroom, they said nothing. Whatever complaints were lodged with the supposed state watchdogs of the court, those were tabled and ignored. It seemed the toxic culture would only spread.

⦿⦿⦿⦿⦿⦿⦿ **CHAPTER 9** ⦿⦿⦿⦿⦿⦿⦿

STANDING UP

⦿⦿⦿⦿⦿⦿⦿⦿⦿⦿⦿⦿⦿⦿⦿⦿⦿⦿⦿⦿⦿⦿⦿

As the scheme ground on, a few truth tellers stood up and howled, to little effect. Several families pleaded for their own child's release and won, without realizing that their single case was but a tiny fraction of a whole. Reporters documented troubling judicial decisions in the courtroom but missed the criminal operation. And some in government who strongly suspected corruption were beaten back by the bullying judges.

One of the first recorded complaints surfaced in 1999, when a thirteen-year-old boy, Anthony, accused of assaulting his little sister, appeared in Judge Mark Ciavarella's courtroom. His mother told the judge their attorney was unable to be in court that day and asked for a postponement. Instead Ciavarella sent Anthony to lockup. His mother called an advocacy group, the Juvenile

Law Center in Philadelphia, the oldest such group in the country. Marsha Levick, the cofounder, took on Anthony's case and won.

"I'll never do it again," Ciavarella told a reporter after the 2001 ruling. "They obviously have a right to a lawyer, and even if they come in and tell me [they] don't want a lawyer, they're going to have one." But the judge failed to keep that public promise.

⛓

As Ciavarella's methods trapped more children and disrupted more families, local reporters noted the wave of confinements. In May of 2004 the *Times Leader* ran a series about Ciavarella's tough-on-crime approach. Reporters spoke to families whose high-performing teens had been detained and come home sullen, angry, and disengaged. The stories revealed harsh treatment at one wilderness camp Ciavarella favored. A reporter described how kids lived the first month at the Adventure Challenge Therapy Camp, formerly Camp Adams, outdoors in a tiny tent village that looked like "an Army surplus refugee center, with low-slung shelters pitched in tight rows on a patch of sand."

In another story, reporter Terrie Morgan-Besecker found that the judge's rate of placing youths outside the home had bounced from 4.5 percent in 1996 to 21 percent in 2002. Luzerne youths were apparently the state's biggest misbehavers, since the county's rate of incarcerating children and youth was higher than anywhere else in Pennsylvania, including Philadelphia and Pittsburgh. And costs to the county had quadrupled, she found.

But the powerful stories gained little traction and the judges carried on.

⛓

In the fall of 2004 an enormous contract materialized for the owners of Pennsylvania Child Care, with President Judge Michael Conahan the broker behind the scenes. The deal would pay the kid-jail owners, Robert Powell and his co-owner, Greg Zappala, $58 million over twenty years, or roughly $3 million per year. And the county would pay another $2 to $3 million annually to a company to manage the center. Later, Pennsylvania Child Care bought that company and received that payment, too.

The county controller, Steve Flood, was stunned by the figures. He was the one who managed the county's wallet, and would later lose reelection. The judges had called him "bombastic" and "a loose cannon" and once tried to jail him for his whistleblowing. Undeterred, Flood insisted that this mega-million-dollar deal begged for transparency. He asked for details and analysis.

Soon, by chance, a powerful voice joined Flood's. A state employee who lived in the county read a newspaper brief about the $58 million deal and sat up straight. Thomas Crofcheck was the state's head whistleblower, or director of auditing for the Department of Public Welfare, the state's largest agency. One of his responsibilities was to monitor state spending in all juvenile facilities, including Pennsylvania Child Care. The news item said the $58 million deal would save money. Highly unlikely, the auditor thought. He remembered another number he'd read, that Pennsylvania Child Care had made a 28 percent profit in its first ten months. Most new businesses were lucky to survive a first year or two, much less turn a profit. A profit in the first ten months? Rare. Pennsylvania Child Care was due for a routine audit anyway. Crofcheck, a certified fraud investigator, decided to move that date up.

As a courtesy, he notified Luzerne County commissioners via several rounds of faxes. They would want to know; he would provide that courtesy. He suggested they hold off on the deal until they could see audit results. But a few days after Crofcheck's notice, the commissioners signed off on the $58-million-over-twenty-years lease.

That didn't stop Crofcheck. When his preliminary draft audit was released to colleagues a month later, his subject line in the cover email summed up his analysis: "Bad Deal."

"It is a bad deal and we get to pay," Crofcheck wrote.

Crofcheck shared a copy with county controller Flood, who leaked the document to the *Times Leader,* which ran a story. The draft audit had plenty to say. Pennsylvania Child Care was charging the highest rates for detaining juveniles in Pennsylvania. It used creative accounting methods, such as switching a youth from one side of the facility, where kids were merely detained without treatment services, to the other side of the facility, where kids were treated for specific conditions on a longer-term basis. and charging a full day's reimbursement twice, once from each side.

In another place or time, Crofcheck's audit might have served as an immediate corrective or forced a sale or shutdown of the detention center. In Luzerne County it worked differently. Pennsylvania Child Care owner Powell contacted Judge Conahan. Conahan advised Powell: file a motion to seal the audit, arguing the need to protect "trade secrets." Powell followed instructions and a hearing was held—in front of Conahan. The president judge prohibited state lawyers from making their argument. He ruled in favor of Pennsylvania Child Care without disclosing his own financial rewards coming from the detention center or Powell's pockets. He sealed the audit, and his arguments for doing so were later described by an appeals court as "drivel."

Still, the decision slammed the lid on further investigation, at least for a while.

By 2005 a few people were getting warmer. Judge Chester Muroski was known as a fair-minded and caring judge who was also unafraid to challenge authority. He had presided over all aspects of family court for many years before Ciavarella arrived in 1996 to take over the juvenile side. Muroski continued with dependency court, where he heard abuse and neglect cases and determined whether children should stay with their families or enter foster care.

Over time Judge Muroski noticed that the county money set aside for his court was shrinking. He shared resources with Ciavarella's juvenile court, and it appeared as if the growing expense of locking up youths in the county had soared. The result was that children from dependency court who had done nothing wrong were languishing for extra months in foster care because the court lacked the money to pay for services that would help families get back together, such as drug and alcohol assessments, parenting classes, and family therapy.

Muroski looked for other money. When he found none, in June of 2005 he wrote a letter to county commissioners, the three elected officials who decided on all county contracts, saying juvenile court was spending a "tremendous amount of money" sending youths away. He said it looked as if the county cared more about locking up kids than it did about protecting abused or neglected children. He requested a meeting.

Three days later, in a letter sent to Muroski's home, President Judge Conahan kicked the sixty-year-old judge from his post of twenty-three years. Muroski was demoted to criminal court, considered a lesser post. He took the new job without a hint of protest, at least then.

But Mary Pat Melvin, a licensed social worker and certified drug addiction counselor, defended Muroski out loud. She had testified in Muroski's courtroom hundreds of times. "Because he tries to do something to help the kids, he was slapped," Melvin dared to say to the *Times Leader*. "I'm furious, absolutely furious."

Melvin didn't know the judge personally. But she knew him to be "very astute" and caring about children. She was risking her own livelihood by speaking out but believed it was time. "Everybody's afraid of retribution," she said. "Everybody's afraid of losing their jobs. Everybody's so afraid."

She continued: "Everybody can play ostrich and stick their heads in the sand, but I couldn't rest with myself if I didn't say something, because this is a very, very wrong move."

In his new post overseeing criminal court, Muroski began seeing pieces of a crime right under his nose: kids appearing without lawyers in Ciavarella's courtroom; upward trends in youths detained; the amazing drain on county money; the "bad deal" leaked audit; widespread nepotism. He also knew about the Florida condo and Robert Powell's private jet and fishing yacht.

Soon after his new assignment, Muroski took a trip to Florida with friends, he later shared with author William Ecenbarger for his 2012 book, *Kids for Cash*. One day, out of curiosity, the group decided to scope out the judges' new condo. Cruising the Jupiter Yacht Club grounds, they were taken aback by the splendor. Conahan had his business interests and had married into money, but Ciavarella came from modest means. How could he afford all this on a judge's salary? Muroski suspected wrongdoing.

Upon his return, Muroski began talking with other judges, including Luzerne County judge Ann Lokuta, who had a head start on Muroski. She was the first woman judge elected to the court in Luzerne County and among the first to suspect Conahan and Ciavarella of being crooks. Cases set to be heard by Lokuta were sometimes snatched away by Conahan and assigned elsewhere, with outcomes that seemed suspiciously favorable to the judges and their allies, Lokuta thought. By speaking out, Lokuta had risen to enemy number one on the judges' retribution list.

By 2006 neither Muroski nor Lokuta had any faith in the state's ability to police Luzerne County. Rumors suggested that a series of complaints about Conahan and Ciavarella were lodged with a secretive state agency meant to police judges, the Judicial Conduct Board. One 2006 anonymous complaint, later circulated, amounted to a comprehensive look at the ugly world inside the Luzerne County Courthouse. The eight-page, single-spaced, highly detailed document named names and identified court cases by their numbers. It described nepotism, links to organized crime, case-fixing, a rise in juvenile admissions to detention centers, and the relationships between Conahan, Ciavarella, and detention center owner Robert Powell. But the Judicial Conduct Board, headed by a Conahan business associate, never investigated the weighty complaint, which amounted to a virtual roadmap to the judges' wrongdoing. They tabled and ignored it, later saying they lacked the resources, prompting a commission to call out the Judicial Conduct Board for protecting judges instead of the citizens of Pennsylvania.

That same year Muroski and Lokuta had at least one thing in common. They each independently took their suspicions to the next level: the FBI.

G.   Attorney Robert Powell is co-owner of the Luzerne County Juvenile Detention Center. When Judge Conahan became President Judge, he assigned Judge Ciaverella to Juvenile Court, while in the past, Juvenile Court responsibilities were shared among Judge Muroski and at times, Judge Lokuta. A stringent pattern of placement in the Powell owned facility can be readily revealed by reviewing Judge Ciavarella's placements. In the past, the other Judges placed in a variety of Facilities including Camp Adams.

H.   Frequently, Judge Conahan, whose closeness to Judge Ciavarella is so great that he purchased a house next to his, will designate Judge Ciaverella to act as President Judge, even though there is no provision for this practice in the Unified Court System of Pennsylvania.

I.   Judge Ciavarella's children have been given access to Attorney Powell's Florida Condo and Judge Conahan and Judge Ciaverella and William Sharkey and the Judges' Staffers have also been given access to Attorney Powell's Condo and to his yatch, "REEL JUSTICE."

J.   Attorney Powell's cases are frequently assigned through order of Judge Conahan to Judge Ciaverella. This task is usually seen to by the Court Administrator, William Sharkey.
Examples of this:

Holling vs. Lovrinic 1733-C-2000
Mancini vs. Rotary Lift 4078-C-2001
Wanser vs. Cannadozza 4771-C-2000
C.T.S.I. vs. MT Marketing 6770-C-2001
Koreyva vs. Eight Bees 2945-C-1999
Sando vs. Fritzengertown 1249-C-1999
Gliem vs. PPL 6184-C-1996

K.   Judge Ciavarella never discloses his close ties to Attorney Powell to either the Litigants or the opposing Counsel. At times, Judge Conahan will also direct cases of Attorney Butera's to Judge Ciavarella, especially when a high profile Plaintiff may be involved who could be linked to Judge Conahan.
Examples of this:

Carpinet vs. Janosky 2619-C-2004
CTSI vs. MT Marketing 6770-C-2001

5

A highly detailed, anonymous complaint filed with the Pennsylvania Judicial Conduct Board in September of 2006 offered a roadmap to criminal activity in the Luzerne County Court of Common Pleas under President Judge Michael Conahan. But the conduct board, headed by a Conahan business associate, tabled the complaint and never investigated.

CHAPTER 10

CRACKS

At fourteen Hillary Transue was shy until she got to talking and then she couldn't stop. She was a bright, sarcastic teen who valued pranks and goofy fun, like dressing up for Halloween as a hot dog in a bun with a squiggle of mustard. Wouldn't it be absolutely hilarious, she and her friends decided in July of 2006, to create a Myspace page mocking their stern and unpopular vice principal? They got to work.

"Hello," began the "About Me" part of the faux social media page. "I am the vice principal of Crestwood High School. I consider myself to be a fun-loving, outgoing individual, who spends most of her time reading silly teen magazines, and daydreaming about Johnny Depp in nothing but tighty whities! Oh la la!"

Next came a call from the police. The officer told Hillary's mother that he was coming to arrest her daughter on charges of terrorism, stalking, and abuse of the internet. Laurene Transue, a veteran social worker, mentioned getting a lawyer. The officer urged her to forego one; if she did he'd reduce the charges to a single count of harassment, which would result in nothing more than probation or community service. Laurene agreed.

The day of her appearance in downtown Wilkes-Barre, Hillary Transue wore a dress and prepared to address the judge with the "yes, sir" and "no, sir" her mother had instructed. Her mother parked the car while Hillary stepped off an elevator at the courthouse annex to face a woman who slid a blank form across a table.

Did she have an attorney? the woman asked.

Hillary said no.

Sign here, she said.

Hillary signed, waiving her legal rights. Upon arrival, her mother signed, too.

Soon mother and daughter stood before Judge Mark Ciavarella, who perused a document and then leaned forward and bellowed: "What makes you think you can get away with this kind of crap?"

"I don't know," Hillary said, backing away, her voice and self shrinking. Her mother put her hand on her shoulder to steady her. "It's okay, it's okay," Laurene Transue whispered in her daughter's ear.

Ciavarella continued in his wizard voice. He had spoken at Hillary's school, Crestwood High. Had she been there that day? Had she heard him speak? What had he said about the consequences of disrespecting teachers and administrators?

"I don't recall, sir," said Hillary.

"You don't recall? You don't?"

"No, sir."

"Were you sleeping?" the judge implored.

"No, sir."

"You can't remember that?"

"No, sir."

"It's going to come back to you because I didn't go to that school, I didn't walk into that school and I didn't speak to that student body just to scare you, just to blow smoke, just to make you think that I would do that when I wouldn't.

"I'm a man of my word!" he snarled. "You're gone."

Ciavarella sentenced Hillary to three months of detention at a girls' wilderness camp. A court employee began shackling Hillary while her mother grew hysterical. This was not what police or probation had promised her, Laurene Transue told the judge. She had never in all her years of social work seen such cruel behavior in a courtroom or as unfitting a sentence.

The court worker, leading Hillary away in chains, hissed at the teen: "Look what you did to your mother!"

∞∞∞

What Hillary actually had done, with her phony Myspace page, was to bring a new round of attention to the domed courthouse on the river. By the time of her court appearance in 2007, angry clouds loomed over the handsome old structure. Federal agents were circling. Courthouse workers traded rumors about who might get caught or go to prison. And the judges and Powell began to step back from their jobs, sell off their holdings, and clear out some bank accounts, as if trying to scrub their fingerprints from a crime scene, grab the money, and run.

In late 2007 President Judge Conahan announced his retirement, at fifty-five, for unspecified "personal reasons." On his way out the door, in January of 2008, Conahan withdrew more than

$302,000 from his pension fund, rather than receiving it in monthly installments. Ciavarella would succeed his close friend as president judge while still running juvenile court, Conahan said.

His stepping back, though, did little to stop the breaking news. Early 2008 brought the final release of a formal and complete government audit—an elaboration on the "bad deal" described in the first draft leaked years earlier. The state supreme court had by then overturned Conahan's "trade secrets" claim, calling it a ruse. But the ruse had helped to stall the audit by four years. Now state auditors said the large sums the county had paid to the detention center could have been used to build at least three county-owned centers. It said inept county officials had allowed Pennsylvania Child Care to reap "unreasonable" profits at taxpayer expense. Powell and his company had earned a 28 percent profit in the first year of operation and a 34 percent profit in the second, the audit noted.

Laurene Transue, meanwhile, distraught and enraged after her daughter's lockup, began agitating to free her. She picked up the phone and dialed: the governor's office, the state public defender's office, the ACLU, Rutgers University, and finally the Juvenile Law Center in Philadelphia, where that group's cofounder, Marsha Levick, took Laurene Transue's call.

To Levick, the call sounded uncannily like the 2001 case of Anthony—the case after which Ciavarella promised never again to hold a hearing for a juvenile who didn't have a lawyer. Levick saw commonalities between the Anthony and Hillary cases: offenses minor, sentences severe, children unrepresented by legal counsel. Despite his early assertions, Ciavarella had not been a man of his word, Levick noted.

After three weeks of Hillary's detention, Levick and the law

Hillary Transue was sent to detention after creating a phony MySpace page mocking an unpopular assistant principal at her high school. Her mother, Laurene Transue, a veteran social worker, contacted the Juvenile Law Center, the oldest advocacy group for juvenile defendants in the country. The Transue case marked the start of a zeroing in on the judges' criminal schemes.

center, arguing that Hillary's constitutional right to a lawyer had been violated, gained her early release. The waiver she had signed getting off the elevator had violated the law.

Then the law center pored over state data. They discovered that the rate of Luzerne youth appearing without lawyers in Ciavarella's courtroom was ten times higher than the state average. Among those unrepresented by counsel, more than half were sent away. The judge's rate of locking up children was two and a half times higher overall than the state average. The cascade of facts amounted to "really, really, very red flags," Levick later said.

In April of 2008 the law center turned to the Pennsylvania Supreme Court. Something was very wrong in Luzerne County. They asked the court to intervene before more harm was done. With their data, sourced from the state's Juvenile Court Judges' Commission, the law center asked the court to immediately review all juvenile cases to identify children and youth who had appeared without counsel, and to dismiss and expunge—erase—their cases from court records.

But the matter of "extraordinary public importance," as put forward by the Juvenile Law Center, produced at the supreme court one more extraordinary silence, prompting speculation about the connection between the detention center co-owner, Gregory Zappala, and the former chief justice of the state supreme court, Stephen Zappala, Greg's father.

The media, in contrast, amplified the news of the law center filing. A round of headlines about the petition hit a public nerve, and in the ensuing days dozens of other distressed families contacted the law center and journalists, including Terrie Morgan-Besecker of the *Times Leader*. She had written about Ciavarella's ruthless methods four years earlier. But with closed juvenile hearings and sealed juvenile records, she had been unaware of violations of kids' legal rights, not to mention the criminal enterprise behind it. Now parents were calling nonstop, each story eerily the same yet told independently. "I swear it was a broken record," the journalist told the documentary filmmakers of *Kids for Cash*. She felt then the frustration of wanting to expose the entire operation to the point of shutting it down. "I wanted to go stand on top of the *Times Leader* building and scream, 'Someone! Look at what's going on here! Someone! Please look at this!'"

Someone *was* looking, as it turned out: the FBI. An agent called Levick. What did she think was going on in Ciavarella's courtroom?

⛓

A picture sharpened as disclosure upon revelation seemed slowly to pry the fifty-two-foot dome a few inches off the courthouse roof. In early May 2008, persuaded by the Juvenile Law Center's compelling data, the state attorney general and the Department of Public Welfare, which licensed detention facilities, joined the law center's petition to the Pennsylvania Supreme Court. And meanwhile Ciavarella's courtroom became circus-like, in one instance drawing a crowd of high school students wearing T-shirts that called for freeing one of their classmates.

Uncharacteristically, Ciavarella released a few youths from detention.

And he resumed defending himself and his courtroom. "Nothing is done unfairly," he told a reporter. No one understood the process—that was the problem. It was probation officers who decided a child's fate, not him. "I don't make the decision that a child gets placed," he asserted. "I just affirm the decision that a child gets placed."

He further insisted that every juvenile was informed three times of their right to counsel—by a police officer, a probation officer, and then by the court with its waiver. If families were informed on three occasions and did nothing, Ciavarella told the *Citizens' Voice*, "I just don't believe I have to spoon feed people to do things in their life." It was their fault.

Then quietly, at the end of May, Ciavarella stepped down as the county's lone juvenile court judge. He had become a distraction, he said, though he would continue as president judge.

If he thought the move might free him from scrutiny, he had misjudged. He and Conahan had, for the first time, listed a few business dealings on 2008 state financial disclosure forms. The forms showed both judges involved in a company that was building eighty-six condominiums in a development they called The Sanctuary, in Mountain Top, where the judges lived. It seemed an incidental point except for one detail: the judges were in business with Robert Powell, owner of the juvenile detention centers and recipient of millions in public money. To anyone already suspicious of the two jurists, like federal prosecutors, here was a connecting puzzle piece. On the last day of May, two county commissioners called for a federal investigation of Powell and the judges.

The news rattled many, including one commissioner who said he was "shocked and absolutely upset" by the financial ties between the judges and Powell. He had voted yes on every funding decision related to the new detention center, from the county's giant $58 million lease deal to another roughly $3 million annual county contract with the management company to operate the centers. Only now had he learned the management company was also owned by Powell.

In the days that followed, Powell sold off his interests in the two juvenile centers and the management company to business partner Zappala. Powell said it was a business decision, having nothing to do with federal probes. By then he and his for-profit kid jails had received more than $30.3 million in payments from state and county funds, records later showed.

Ciavarella, meanwhile, sold his Mountain Top home, gave the proceeds to his daughter to buy a new home, and moved in with family.

⊂⊃⊂⊃

In late June the federal government raided the Luzerne County Probation Department, seizing records of billing statements related to Pennsylvania Child Care and the numbers of youths detained there. In August the feds served subpoenas on three higher-up staff at the courthouse. Money had gone missing. Tens of thousands of dollars seized from illegal gambling operations throughout the county had come into the court's possession, but the money never arrived at the district attorney's office where it belonged. The day after the subpoenas, one of those employees, William Sharkey, Conahan's cousin, the court administrator in charge of courthouse books, took an indefinite paid sick leave.

Also in June, county commissioners decided to dismiss Dr. Frank Vita, the juvenile court psychologist and Conahan's brother-in-law. Auditors learned he'd earned more than $1.1 million in county funds. A typical salary for the job was $70,000 to $100,000 annually. Vita's ranged from $180,000 to $234,000. In 2004, for the hours documented and the county salary he received, he would've had to have worked 49.9 hours a week for fifty-two weeks, auditors said. The county would likely have to repay the state hundreds of thousands of dollars for his overbilling.

The courthouse subpoenas signaled another fact: people were being summoned to testify to a federal grand jury, a group of citizens selected to hear evidence to determine whether federal crimes had been committed and formal charges needed to be filed.

By the fall of 2008, rumors had reached a feverish pitch in the courthouse, newspaper headlines said, but it was premature to expect that anyone would be charged with crimes. An editorial suggested, drily, that the FBI might want to set up a branch office in the courthouse. An anti-tax activist later insisted that, in anticipation of a courthouse centennial, there ought to be a cleanup of the corruption and greed inside that had gone unchecked for the past 100 years. Instead of a party, said the activist, Gene Stilp, who hauled a 26-foot inflated pink pig outside of the building to protest the shady dealings, there should be "a week-long ethics ceremony for everyone that works in there."

∞

In December of 2008 the Juvenile Law Center, having heard nothing from the Pennsylvania Supreme Court, filed an amended version of their emergency petition, the one asking the court for an immediate examination of Ciavarella's cases. The law center said it was trying again because little had changed in Luzerne County, except for a lengthening list of youths whose lives had been upended. A few days later, in early January of 2009, the law center finally heard back.

The state's highest court, in a one-page decision without explanation, denied the petition.

CHAPTER 11

CAT AND MOUSE

On a clear July day in 2008, three conspiring men met in an empty townhouse complex in Mountain Top to talk about how to keep their stories straight should they be charged with crimes. As they spoke, Judge Mark Ciavarella wandered over to a kitchen window and peered outside. There in the parking lot he spotted a plain-looking blue van. Was it a contractor's commercial vehicle? Were the feds watching and listening? Was either of his pals wearing a wire? Was he paranoid?

Throughout that summer, a cat-and-mouse game had escalated as the federal government closed in on the scheming judges and the judges in turn kept track of the circling feds. Investigators were digging through file cabinets, seizing documents and ledgers, scouring bank accounts, and delivering witness names to a grand jury. It was part of a continuing probe of corruption in Luzerne County that would eventually snag dozens of county workers. "You could work these cases for years," said the head of the defunct Pennsylvania Crime Commission, which investigated organized crime in the state. "Every time you turn over one rock, another seven lizards crawl out."

But as the feds got closer, the highly connected judges followed the investigators' moves. From those bits and pieces, they tried to line up their own lies to create one story, for an impenetrable mutual defense.

ꝍꝍꝍ

Federal investigators had kicked off their probe when FBI agents, surveilling Mafia boss William "Big Billy" D'Elia, were led to his breakfasts with Judge Michael Conahan. From there, like a TV crime script, the feds followed the money. They gained access to Conahan's bank accounts, tax returns, lists of assets, and state financial disclosure statements. It was unglamorous, mind-numbing detective work, but it produced ironclad evidence. Agents traced Conahan funds to the Pinnacle Group of Jupiter. They wondered why the president judge had received gobs of money and why it had landed at Pinnacle. "Then we see [this company] is jointly held by Conahan's and Ciavarella's wives," recalled Michael Consiglio, the assistant US attorney for the Middle District of Pennsylvania who worked the case. "Then we knew, they're hiding something here."

They traced Pinnacle deposits backward—to Robert Powell.

Soon the feds were examining Powell's own sprawling financial picture, which included the sums he had sent by wire and check to Pinnacle. Where had all *that* money come from?

Armed with the hard evidence, IRS agents in 2007 dropped in on Powell at his luxury manse in Mountain Top, where he lived with his wife and three children in lavish Powell style. His 7,500-square-foot, newly constructed manor sat on five acres and featured a pool, a tennis court, a guesthouse over a garage, and a recreation center with a basketball court.

At the compound, the federal agents laid out the Byzantine financial transactions right in front of Powell. And they told him that if he cooperated with the government against the judges, he could save himself from lengthy prison time. "They indicated on the down-low that he could make [his] situation better," said Consiglio. Powell agreed to help.

The judges, meanwhile, sensing doom, continued embroidering their defense as they heard new leaks from the grand jury. In early 2008 they contacted Powell for a nighttime meeting behind Crestwood High, one of the schools where Ciavarella had spoken to student assemblies about zero tolerance and from which students were later funneled to his courtroom. Conahan picked up Powell in a late-model sedan and Ciavarella sat in the passenger seat with Powell in back. Driving backroads in the area, the two judges told Powell the latest from the grand jury. Builder Mericle had testified falsely that Powell was the orchestrator of the million-dollar payments. Powell's law partner, Jill Moran, had told the grand jury about delivering cash-stuffed boxes to the courthouse at Powell's request. How could the three men in the car address Mericle's and Moran's testimony? All three would need to tell the same lies. "Bobby, you've got to hold the water here," Ciavarella instructed Powell, Powell later said under oath. "You've got to say those boxes never came to us."

The three men entered into a "mutual defense agreement," a Three Musketeers, all-for-one-and-one-for-all pact that formalized their joint defense, even though Powell had already made his deal, behind their backs, to cooperate with the federal government.

❦❦❦

In six meetings that summer Powell taped a tiny microphone to his chest and met with the judges. In an early meeting Powell confided his worry that his business partner, Gregory Zappala, hearing about the grand jury, had become suspicious of Powell's hand in the cash drawers of the two juvenile detention centers. As they spoke Zappala was scouring the books, trying to figure out where all the money had gone, Powell told Conahan. Now Powell feared Zappala would sue him. That would allow Zappala to see Powell's law-firm books, which would reveal the exact route the monies had taken. It would show how Powell had pulled money from the detention centers, deposited it with his law firm, and then turned the money into withdrawals in checks, wires, and cash to Pinnacle and the judges.

"So what are you saying?" Conahan asked Powell in one early meeting. The recordings were later played in court.

"It's where the cash came from," Powell said.

"Well, there's nothing we can do about that," Conahan said. "If [Zappala] files a suit he files a suit."

"But that puts us in an untenable position," Powell said.

"In what way?"

"Well, what if they put me under oath?"

"Well, they're gonna," Conahan said. Powell's law partner,

Moran, had already told the grand jury about carrying boxes of cash to the courthouse, Conahan reminded Powell.

"Okay," Conahan continued. "Let me tell you something. If you want to check me, I'm not wearing a wire."

"Neither am I," lied the wired Powell.

Conahan said it was vital to get their stories straight. "Bob, I'm going to tell you something right now," Conahan warned. "This is my story. I'm never changing this story. I leased you that [Florida condo)]for fifteen grand a month for sixty months."

Conahan stressed that he would never admit to having received any cash payments from any person or company: "Tell you one thing right now. I never lied to you and I never will. I'd never do anything to hurt you but I never got the cash from anybody. That's the story. And you better stick to it."

"I'll stick to it," Powell assured Conahan.

A few minutes later Conahan reiterated: "Bobby, if there's anything coming out of [a Powell company] or PA [Pennsylvania] Child Care—cash—you just gotta say it didn't come to me."

"All right," Powell said.

"When this is all done," Conahan assured Powell, "whatever we have to sit down to work it out or help each other, we'll do it."

oⴰⴰo

In the final recording, on that hot summer day in late July of 2008, the judges and Powell met at The Sanctuary, the eighty-six-unit condominium complex they had tried and eventually failed to develop. There, inside the model unit, they described what they knew about the FBI probe and tried once more to solidify a defense. They discussed paying off Powell's business partner, Greg Zappala, but Powell said it wouldn't work. Zappala would be unswayed by money. They discussed ways to discredit Robert Mericle, the developer. They talked about the problematic Jill Moran, who had delivered the boxes to the courthouse but was now ghosting the men, meaning she was certainly cooperating with authorities.

Conahan insisted once more on coordinating stories. "Listen," Conahan said, "you paid me rent for my condo. You didn't pay me rent for my condo to shut the juvenile detention center down or fix cases."

About the cash boxes, Conahan repeated: "And I got no boxes from [Jill]. Nobody gave boxes to [Jill]. If somebody gave boxes to [Jill], she has them."

᚛᚜

And then, all at once, Ciavarella stood up and walked to the kitchen window. "Shhhhhh," he said and gestured toward the blue van outside.

Powell swore and said they had better go. The three men walked outside. Two stayed back while Ciavarella approached the van. He tried peering through the darkened windows.

Inside the van FBI agent James Glenn and a colleague had been listening in on, and recording, the men's conversation via Powell's wire. As Ciavarella approached, Glenn shut down the surveillance, fearing the humming sound of devices would give them away. The agents held their breath. "We could actually hear him [Ciavarella] approaching," Glenn later testified, "the footsteps, closer, closer to the van, grasping the handle of the front passenger door trying to get in. Moving around the van to the back door, trying to get in, the side door, to the front door, but he was unsuccessful."

Then Ciavarella returned to his friends, apparently reassured, since he later made one more forty-thousand-dollar demand of

Powell, Powell later said. This time Powell had a different answer. "I don't have $40,000 and if I did, I wouldn't give it to you," Powell later testified about the exchange. "This is over."

The three men left The Sanctuary that day and sped off in different directions. Agent Glenn stayed behind for another fifteen minutes, then left with a heap of incriminating evidence.

CHAPTER 12

TERRIBLE, HORRIBLE, NO GOOD

Dread hung over the Luzerne County Courthouse in the opening days of 2009. Federal agents had raided offices and subpoenaed witnesses, yet no one had been charged. Then, on the morning of January 26, an announcement ripped through town. The court explained that Mark Ciavarella would step down as president judge but remain on the bench.

That afternoon, at a news conference, federal prosecutors described an illegal scheme. Ciavarella, then fifty-eight, and

Michael Conahan, by then called a "senior judge" because he continued to hear cases on a per diem basis, had been working behind the scenes to use their judgeships like cash machines—by jailing children and youths who had appeared in juvenile court, then pocketing government reimbursements while trying to hide the cash. The two men had received at least $2.8 million in kickbacks, or illegal payments.

A complaint laid out the government's case: Conahan had singlehandedly shut down the old juvenile detention center and then created and signed a phony lease agreement in order to persuade a bank to lend money to build a new one. Ciavarella had filled the kid jails with children even against his own probation officers' recommendations. And the judges had pushed lease agreements with the county worth tens of millions of dollars—and then Powell had pocketed large sums for himself and paid off the judges.

The judges had agreed to plead guilty to corrupt practices and serve eighty-seven months in prison, or about seven years, the government said. The men would pay restitution in an amount to be determined. They would resign from office and be disbarred. But they would need to formally enter their guilty pleas in court.

That day came on February 12, 2009, a "terrible, horrible, no good, very bad day" for the judges, wrote Dave Janoski, a *Citizens' Voice* reporter, borrowing from the title of a popular children's book. There were fingerprints and mugshots. TV cameras followed the disgraced men, who were dressed up in dark suits and wearing grim looks.

Some eighty people filled the Scranton courtroom, with another forty or so watching via a closed-circuit TV nearby. Senior US District Judge Edwin M. Kosik asked a series of legal questions. The county ex-judges answered: "No, your honor," and "Yes, your honor," and then "Guilty, your honor," when asked to enter their pleas.

They surrendered their passports and were released on bail, backed by the lavish Florida condo that had helped them launder their cash. And then they hustled silently out of the federal courthouse and pressed through and around a mob of reporters to whom they had no comment. Getting into waiting SUVs, they tried to escape bystanders' angry jeers. Why weren't *they* being led off to locked cells wrapped in shackles, one mother wondered aloud. Others screamed at the fallen jurists:

"Where's the robe at?"

"Burn in hell!"

"You Pigs!"

⛓

Watchdogs shifted into a higher gear. The unstoppable Juvenile Law Center tried a third time with the unmovable Pennsylvania Supreme Court. Two days later the court, finally pressed or shamed into action after the federal charges, agreed to look at Luzerne County's juvenile cases. They appointed Senior Judge Arthur Grim, a respected veteran juvenile court judge from another county, as a special master to review all Ciavarella juvenile cases.

Reporters excavated the judges' histories. They tied Conahan definitively to a convicted felon, a drug dealer who had become a named guest at the Jupiter condo and ran a Florida car dealership with Conahan's wife. They also connected Conahan to mob boss William "Big Billy" D'Elia and raised the possibility that the judges were fixing cases at D'Elia's behest. D'Elia vigorously denied that claim while testimony later suggested otherwise. But those charges were never proven by the government.

Reporters revealed how Ciavarella on the bench, vicious with children, had a light touch with some adults. In 2003 he showed mercy to a coal company heir after the man, Louis Pagnotti III, abducted three children who were inside a car that he stole while having a psychotic episode. Ciavarella gave Pagnotti probation.

Reporters from the Philadelphia-based *Legal Intelligencer* looked up all cases where lawyer Robert Powell had argued in front of Judge Ciavarella. Multimillion-dollar verdicts and settlements in favor of Powell and his clients added up to about $16.5 million in total. One defense lawyer, suspicious of the cascade of Ciavarella's rulings against him and in favor of Powell, even asked the judge at the time whether he had any conflicts of interest in regard to Powell. Ciavarella just got mad. But many other attorneys on the losing end of Ciavarella's rulings began asking for new trials. "Imagine learning at your state champ soccer match that the other team had paid the referee a million bucks," said assistant US Attorney Mike Consiglio. "And [the referee] is hoping to get millions more. You're going to lose your mind. The playing field is totally slanted."

In February William Sharkey, Conahan's brother-in-law and the court administrator, was charged with stealing seventy thousand dollars in seized county gambling money.

In July Robert Powell pled guilty to helping the judges disguise the kickbacks they received and failing to report to authorities that the judges had lied. He agreed to forfeit his fishing yacht and tricked-out jet. He would pay more than $4.75 million toward a fund for children and continue to cooperate with the government.

The state cut off the judges' salaries. Eventually they lost their pensions. Then Luzerne County waited for the plea deal to become final and for the judges to go to jail. The government had only to conduct a presentence investigation, results of which would help the federal judge decide whether to sign off. Columnists, reflecting on the fates of the judges, referenced an old game show: *Deal or No Deal.*

CHAPTER 13

RAGE AND SORROW

One day in the winter of Elizabeth Habel's fourteenth year, officials at her high school called her parents to say that Elizabeth was drunk. The Habels needed to pick up their daughter, take her home, and sober her up. When Gloria and Richard Habel arrived, they found Elizabeth handcuffed in the back of a police cruiser, sobbing. She had been sexually assaulted, she said. Her friend, also intoxicated, explained that the assault had occurred a few weeks earlier, and it had taken Elizabeth's excessive drinking to help her blurt out what had happened. Later she testified against her assailant and he went to prison.

But on the next February day in 2006, Elizabeth Habel wound up in Judge Mark Ciavarella's juvenile courtroom, where he threw Elizabeth into detention. From that moment forward a painful saga played out in the Habel family, as Elizabeth cycled through institutions and her family fought to free her.

Three years later, as news of judicial corruption jolted the region and traveled the world, the Habels and others stepped forward. Local radio call-ins radiated public anger. The *New York Times*, in its Quotation of the Day, featured a Luzerne mother, her son once detained, speaking after the judges' hearing. "It was nice to see them sitting on the other side of the bench." Another mother told a local newspaper, "He sat there calling my daughter a criminal while all along on that bench *he* was the criminal."

Over the next months many more Luzerne residents stepped forward in a #MeToo-like wave. Ambulance-chasing trial lawyers from across the country tried to take advantage by taking out ads in local newspapers to solicit clients. Reporters uncovered more bizarre or outrageous stories: A young man who stole a four-dollar bottle of nutmeg spent seven months at three facilities; a seventeen-year-old youth was shackled for more than thirteen hours while transported from one place to the next; a young woman, in a dispute over a candy bar, hit her mother with a pillow. Ciavarella sentenced her to fifty-six days at Camp Adams, where she met girls charged with assault, auto theft, and drug dealing. "Then there was me, the pillow batterer," she told a reporter. To this day, some high school classmates "still believe I stabbed my mom." And Gloria, Richard, and Elizabeth Habel went public with their rage. Their contact with juvenile justice had started over a rock-throwing game in 2005. That's when the young teen Elizabeth Habel, her sister, and a friend from across the street had made up a game to see who could throw a rock over a telephone wire in Plymouth, a small coal town near Wilkes-Barre. Elizabeth hurled a rock over the wire, she said, and on the way down it struck her neighbor. A police report said the 11-year-old girl suffered a large gash in her lip, required several stitches, and suffered nerve damage to two teeth. The Habels said it was an accident, and Gloria and Elizabeth baked brownies together and took them to the neighbors and apologized. The children stayed close after that, playing together nearly every day.

But five or six months later, in 2005, the Habels received an order from the Luzerne County Juvenile Court to appear on the rock-throwing matter. The neighbors were bringing charges. Soon Elizabeth was in court, listening to her friend's mother tell Judge Ciavarella that Elizabeth had deliberately thrown a rock at her daughter's face, chipping a front tooth.

Taken aback, Elizabeth tried to explain. The rock was more like a pebble and she had tossed it over the wire in a game. "Your honor, it was an honest-to-god accident," she said.

No, the judge said, Elizabeth had an anger problem. Ciavarella judged her "delinquent" for a "simple assault" and placed her on "indefinite strict probation." That meant a six p.m. home curfew, random drug testing in school, and community service. Elizabeth, a straight-A student, often raced home to meet her curfew and missed a few, and so was issued an electronic ankle monitor. That felt like a branding. The punishments felt unfair and indefinite. When would probation end?

"She didn't see any light at the end of the tunnel," her mother, Gloria Habel, later said under oath. "She totally went right off the wall. And by that I mean she was facing a lot of depression, a lot of anger issues because she didn't feel like it was right. She started running away."

The day after she was found intoxicated at school, Judge Ciavarella sent her to Pennsylvania Child Care, where she was greeted by a woman carrying jailhouse sandals and clothing. She ordered Elizabeth to strip, and Elizabeth stood naked while the woman examined and jotted down every scar on her body. Then she watched Elizabeth shower and get dressed.

Elizabeth was led to a cinderblock cell with a metal desk and bed bolted to the concrete floor. The only daylight shone through a narrow opaque window against the back wall. The high ceiling was stuck with spitballs, and Elizabeth feared they might drop on top of her when she slept.

Elizabeth spent many weeks sitting alone in the room. With a pencil and paper, she drew childish hearts and declarations of love to her parents. "I [heart] you both," one drawing said. Another shows her own face and her parents encircled by a large heart with a title, "My Loving Family."

On the day Elizabeth was to be sentenced, the Habels tried visiting Ciavarella before their daughter's court appearance. He needed to know that Elizabeth had been raped—that was why she had been acting out. The couple found a man making coffee in his chambers. When they realized it was Ciavarella, they shared Elizabeth's history.

"It does not matter," Ciavarella told them, Gloria Habel later recounted under oath. "She has to pay for what she did, and do not mention it in my courtroom."

Richard Habel added: "He said, 'Do not say [anything] in my courtroom about that. She has to be held accountable for her actions.' Those were his exact words to us."

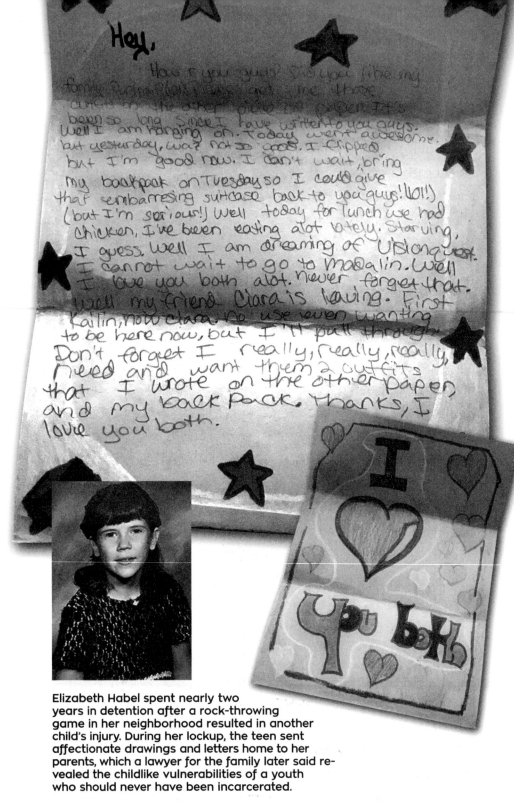

Hey,

Have you guys? Did you like my family picture and the those cuter in the other piece of paper. It's been so long since I have written to you guys. Well I am hanging on. Today went awesome, but yesterday, was not so good. I flipped but I'm good now. I can't wait, bring my backpack on Tuesday so I could give that embarressing suitcase back to you guys! (lol!) (but I'm serious!) Well today for lunch we had chicken, I've been eating alot lately. Starving, I guess. Well I am dreaming of Ublonquist. I cannot wait to go to mabalin. Well I love you both alot. never forget that. Well my friend Ciara is leaving. First Kailin, now Ciara. no use even wanting to be here now, but I'll pull through. Don't forget I really, really, really, need and want them 2 outfits that I wrote on the other paper, and my back pack. Thanks, I love you both.

Elizabeth Habel spent nearly two years in detention after a rock-throwing game in her neighborhood resulted in another child's injury. During her lockup, the teen sent affectionate drawings and letters home to her parents, which a lawyer for the family later said revealed the childlike vulnerabilities of a youth who should never have been incarcerated.

Later that day Ciavarella sent Elizabeth back to detention to await a psychological evaluation. The day of the review, the Habels learned Elizabeth had been switched into another cell just vacated by a young woman with hepatitis B. "They did not switch the toothbrushes," Gloria Habel testified. "Nobody told her [Elizabeth] the toothbrushes were not switched, and she used that toothbrush. She was hysterical." It took three months before Elizabeth learned she was negative for hepatitis B.

Then one day in March the phone rang at the Habel home. A probation officer from VisionQuest, a bootcamp-style detention center for troubled kids, was welcoming the entire family to the program after the hearing that morning.

"Whoa, whoa, whoa," Gloria Habel interrupted. "What the heck are you talking about? What hearing?" Ciavarella had sentenced Elizabeth to the treatment center without a lawyer or her parents present, the worker told her.

When, several weeks later, the Habels visited Elizabeth, they were alarmed. She had been given a powerful cocktail of medications that caused her hands to twitch and her vision to blur. She was undergoing intense physical training with drill-sergeant-type staff who issued harsh commands, standing so close she could smell their breath. One weekend in May her parents arrived to emergency vehicles surrounding the facility. Some girls had put rocks into socks and attacked the staff, they learned. Visiting was cancelled. The Habels turned around and drove the four hours home.

Elizabeth was sent to two more placements over the next two years. During that time she was restrained in an upper body hold and thrown to the ground by staff. Her mother called child welfare officials. Why were the Habels forbidden to hug, kiss, or otherwise touch their daughter, yet staff could manhandle her as they wished?

Gloria Habel contacted child advocates, state watchdogs, and government offices. Finally an aide to a state senator arranged a meeting with probation department staff at the Luzerne County Courthouse.

The next day, in early January of 2008, Ciavarella released Elizabeth Habel. In her two years of lockup, she had received no treatment for the sexual assault. Now with the judges' own guilty pleas, the Habels understood the context that helped explain their daughter's ordeal. They shared with a reporter Ciavarella's last belittling words.

"Elizabeth, I know you're going to mess up. I have no faith in you whatsoever," said Ciavarella, Elizabeth Habel relayed to a reporter about a year later. "You're going to end up in my courtroom again and I'm going to end up sending you away. I'm the one who's going to have the last laugh."

CHAPTER 14

DEAL OR
NO DEAL

The public waited for justice while the judges behaved according to temperament: one talked nonstop, the other shut down. Both were defiant. Michael Conahan retreated into seclusion while filing objections to the plea deal. Mark Ciavarella created a collage of contradictory public words. Judge Edwin Kosik watched and waited.

In March of 2009 reporter Jim Avila of ABC News ambushed Ciavarella in a parking lot as the judge, dressed in a navy hooded sweatshirt with a cellphone to his ear, stepped out of a light blue station wagon. "Hang on, I'll call you back," Ciavarella said into the phone. Avila introduced himself, and the men shook hands with cameras rolling.

"You know," began Avila, "a lot of people are wondering how a man of such distinction like yourself could've gotten in so much trouble and sold these kids down the river."

"Well, let's stop right there," Ciavarella interrupted, raising a finger at Avila. "I didn't sell any kids down the river."

Avila produced a document outlining the charges against Ciavarella.

Yes, right, the ex-judge said. He had admitted to some charges but not all. "I'm not pleading guilty to anything relative to cash for kids, embezzlement, extortion, quid pro quo. Absolutely not."

Avila asked about the rapid-fire hearings for kids without attorneys.

"That's not true; that's not true," Ciavarella said, his eyeglasses turning darker in the bright light. The probation staff decided a child's fate, lockup or probation. He merely rubber-stamped the decisions, he said.

Avila asked Ciavarella about the children and families who felt unjustly condemned.

"You take a look at their file," Ciavarella said, with another emphatic jab of his finger, "and you look to see if this was the first time they had a run-in with the law. . . . You may be surprised that it's not going to be as clear-cut as they would like you to think."

Reporter Avila later fact-checked Ciavarella's words with Judge Arthur E. Grim, the special master appointed by the state supreme court to examine hundreds of Ciavarella's cases and transcripts. Grim said Ciavarella had violated professional practice. For one, Ciavarella often ignored his probation staff's recommendations, sending kids to probation when probation had recommended the child go home. And in any case, "You have no business reading those [probation] reports," said Grim, who also chaired the Pennsylvania Juvenile Court Judges' Commission. "You don't want to be tainted by somebody else's impression of a child. You want to try the case based on the facts."

And Grim said the kids were good kids, not criminals. "The kids were in there for relatively minor first-time offenses and ended up being placed," Grim told Avila. "The judge is incorrect."

Avila asked Grim why this case mattered, given the many instances of corruption exposed every day across the country.

"It's kids," said the senior judge, shaking his head. "I'm sorry," he added, fighting off upset during a camera close-up. He tried again. "It really . . ." He chuckled at his own discomposure and struggled to shake it off. "Damn it—it really upsets me because it's on the back of kids, and that's unfair."

He added, "Talk about a bad lesson."

ᴄᴐᴄᴐ

A few months later Ciavarella incriminated himself when he was called to defend a suspicious court decision he had made while a judge. In a newspaper libel case, Ciavarella had ruled against the *Citizen's Voice*—in favor of a local businessman who traveled in social circles with mobster William "Big Billy" D'Elia and Judge Michael Conahan. The newspaper, in light of federal charges against the judges, had appealed the decision. They said the case had been fixed. To prove it, they called a witness who knew everyone involved, including the man who had won the $3.5 million libel award, Thomas Joseph, a local businessman. Joseph had filed the original lawsuit because he said the newspaper damaged his reputation with stories that connected him to Mafia boss D'Elia.

The newspaper's new witness, Robert Kulick, testified in a new hearing. He said he was friendly with the now ex-judges, Ciavarella and Conahan, with the complaining businessman, Joseph, and with D'Elia, the mob boss who had the breakfast meetings with Conahan. Kulick, an associate of D'Elia, testified that he sometimes joined the unofficial breakfast club, and he told the court what D'Elia had confided to him: in the libel case, Joseph was sure to win. "According to him [D'Elia], he knew Tommy Joseph was going to win the case," Kulick said under oath. "And we laughed about it."

Kulick also wrote a sworn declaration to the court: "On several occasions, D'Elia told me that he had discussed the Joseph case with Judge Conahan, that Judge Conahan had told him he had discussed the case with Judge Ciavarella, and that the outcome of the case was going to be positive for Joseph."

⊂⊃⊂⊃

Joseph's team, in turn, called Ciavarella as a witness, to defend his $3.5 million decision. "The words poured out of Mark A. Ciavarella Jr. like sweat on that warm afternoon," wrote Michael Sisak of the Citizens' Voice, "fragments of truth and excuses interspersed with the arrogance and defiance that defined his time as a judge."

Sisak wrote that Ciavarella "turned his cross-examination into an exercise of catharsis and confession." Ciavarella admitted that he had been a corrupt judge. He had received hundreds of thousands of dollars in hidden cash related to the juvenile detention centers. He had lied on his taxes and in his state financial disclosure forms. Still, Ciavarella told the appeals court, the payments were merely a "finder's fee," not an illegal kickback. "I did not consider what

I did to be illegal," he told the court. "I did not consider the money that I was receiving to be illegal mob money. I was told it was something that I was entitled to."

The judge who presided over the appeal, William H. Platt, ordered a new trial. He said Ciavarella's testimony added to evidence that the libel case had been fixed. "Tellingly," Platt wrote, "former Judge Ciavarella, a witness called by [Joseph], was, because of his demeanor and lack of remorse, one of [the newspaper's] best witnesses."

∞

Meanwhile, Federal Judge Kosik was dismayed. Ciavarella's interview and court testimony in the libel case had presented a mishmash of admissions, denials, and self-contradictions. Both Ciavarella and Conahan had filed piles of objections to the plea deal and denied taking any money. Ciavarella said he had thought the millions he received were legal, though he tried to hide the money. And the close-mouthed Conahan failed to take responsibility for his actions when he spoke to investigators. How did any of that amount to sincere admissions of guilt?

On July 31 of 2009, Kosik scrapped the deal.

"We paraphrase what has been written about judges," Kosik wrote in his unexpected decision, "that, above all things, integrity is their lot and proper virtue, the landmark, and he that removes it, corrupts the fountain. In this case, the fountain from which the public drinks is confidence in the judicial system—a fountain which may be corrupted for a time well after this case."

CHAPTER 15

DEPTHS OF INDIFFERENCE

With the deal undone, the judges withdrew their pleas and their attorneys pointed out that their legal status had flipped—from guilty to innocent until proven guilty. But that wouldn't last, as the case had finally activated other arms of government. In August Judge Arthur Grim, the special master appointed by the state supreme court, recommended that the court vacate and expunge records of at least 2,400 youths who had come before Ciavarella between 2003 and 2008. Grim documented that Ciavarella had jailed juveniles on minor charges, failed to fully inform them of their rights, and pressured or overruled probation officers in order to lock up kids.

In September of 2009 the region was stunned once more, this time by the federal grand jury, the body of citizens convened by federal prosecutors to review evidence about the judges. They produced a forty-eight-count indictment charging both men with using the courts to enrich themselves by $2.8 million. The duo pled not guilty.

And during the same period the state legislature created the Interbranch Commission on Juvenile Justice to find out what had gone wrong in Luzerne County and how to fix it. The commission held eleven days of hearings and interviewed sixty-eight witnesses, including a few who praised Ciavarella. "The man you're describing as a monster came in every day and greeted his staff," said Angela Zera, a probation supervisor, "talked to us more often than not about the job being a vocation to help children. He took time to sidebar and console and hug parents, and he went to see these kids graduate. He helped them get into college."

That would be a minority view. Robert Schwartz, cofounder of the Juvenile Law Center and an expert on juvenile justice, presented a scorching summary of a juvenile court gone rogue. "Luzerne County was a toxic combination of for-profit facilities, corrupt judges, and professional indifference," he told the commission. Referring to an infamous environmental disaster of the 1970s, Schwartz added, "It was the Love Canal of juvenile courts."

The judges used kids to make money and nobody seemed to notice. "Imagine if judges were openly selling stolen goods in the courtroom," Schwartz told the eleven-member commission, made up of state judges, heads of probation, and district attorneys. "You can bet that professionals in the room would have blown the whistle in a second. But summarily moving shackled kids from the courtroom to the cell room didn't bother anyone."

Schwartz posed the mysterious question: how could so many have born witness for so long and done nothing? "Prosecutors, defenders, other lawyers, probation staff—all claimed to be at the unlit periphery of this scandal," Schwartz said. "Sometimes though what happens at the periphery is the heart of the matter. It took an unprecedented breadth and depth of indifference by all of these individuals to allow the Luzerne County scandal to occur."

He quoted author Amy Bach, an expert on systemic failures in criminal courts: "Ordinary injustice results when a community of legal professionals become[s] so accustomed to a pattern of lapses that they can no longer see their role in them."

Schwartz's cofounder, Marsha Levick, later wondered aloud about the overwhelming failure of so many to see and speak up, from the Judicial Conduct Board and state supreme court to a community of legal professionals in the courtroom and finally to the many families who suffered in silence. To Levick, the conduct board and supreme court were incapable of policing their own. The professionals in the courtroom likely feared for their jobs and then, as author Bach wrote, became accustomed and numb.

And families had their own reasons: "I think community silence—the parents, the families—was driven more from a feeling of powerlessness that comes from being in an economically disadvantaged community," Levick said of the mostly white families without vast resources, connections, or know-how to fight back.

The case, she said, illuminates the caste system in juvenile justice. Black and brown youths comprise some 70 percent of offenders in the US juvenile justice system. In Wilkes-Barre, the thousands who had the misfortune of coming before the court were overwhelmingly white. Experts lament that a case involving mostly white kids received such widespread attention while similar, more numerous instances involving children and youth of color may go unnoticed. "It's impossible to talk about 'kids for cash' and not acknowledge that we are talking largely about a white community," said Levick. "I think many people, from different backgrounds, said if this had been a community of color, the types of kids we typically see in most of the juvenile justice system, would we have paid as close attention? And what does that say?"

Shining a light on Luzerne County reveals a broken system, she said. "And those things that are broken for white kids are broken for black and brown kids, too, with worse repercussions. Race is an important part of the conversation."

What the saga did reveal was that poorer families with fewer advantages saw their children shackled and sent away, while the sons and daughters of people with influence—with the means and sophistication to contact competent lawyers, news reporters or youth advocates—were more likely to be spared any consequence at all. Some have called it coal cracker justice.

"I don't like your kind," is what the chief probation officer in Luzerne County told Susan Morgans and her daughter, Kelcy, when they first reported to the department after a drug test found a scant amount of marijuana in Kelcy's system, Susan Morgans said. "We don't like people like you."

ᴄᴏᴏ

The Interbranch Commission, in its final report released in May of 2010, also emphasized the mass silence that enveloped the Luzerne County Courthouse. It pointed fingers at two district attorneys who had never set foot in juvenile court during their entire careers, and at the chief public defender who had failed to monitor his assistants. Through his silence his office had become utterly complicit.

The commission produced a report with many recommendations, most implemented, from changed judicial ethics procedures to better training for prosecutors, new laws barring children's waiving of counsel, simpler procedures for children to appeal, and easier expungement of juvenile records. No child is shackled, unless a danger to himself or others.

ᏩᏭᎠ

The legal system ground on. In July ex-judge Michael Conahan switched his plea to guilty on a charge of racketeering, a crime of engaging in illegal business activities with others. He would later be sentenced to seventeen years in federal prison. The ever-combative Ciavarella, shocked by what he perceived as betrayal by his close friend Conahan, continued to trial. His day in court came in February of 2011, when, following ten days of proceedings with testimony from Robert Mericle, Robert Powell, and finally ex-judge Ciavarella, a jury found him guilty of twelve of thirty-nine felonies.

Moments later Ciavarella walked out of the courthouse with his attorney, Al Flora, and into a chaotic gaggle of reporters, photographers, and TV cameras at the top of the courthouse steps. "How do you feel, Al?" a reporter called out.

"We're amazed," Flora began in low tones as cameras clicked in staccato and a dog barked in the background. "The jury rejected ninety-five percent of the government's case. . . . They rejected most of the theories regarding kickbacks and bribes. The government really got hurt today in this entire case. And it stands for the proposition that what Mark Ciavarella said all along was true: he never took a kickback, he never took a bribe, and he never extorted Robert Powell!" Flora's tone popped at the word "Powell," then climbed to a growly, emphatic register: "And the government affirmed him on all three things! *This is not a cash for kids case! And we hope . . ."*

"Oh, it wasn't?" shouted a woman's voice in the background.

Flora continued ". . . *somebody starts getting the message!"*

"'Cause my kid's not *here* anymore!" exclaimed the woman, Sandy Fonzo, the mother of a teen who appeared before Ciavarella for carrying drug paraphernalia. Her son was Edward R. Kenzakoski III, an all-star high-school wrestler who spent time in juvenile detention and then state prison. He shot himself in 2010 at the

This iconic photo of Sandy Fonzo, captured after a February 2011 jury verdict in the criminal case against Mark Ciavarella, came to symbolize the rage and grief endured by many families whose children passed through juvenile court during the judge's tenure. Ciavarella was found guilty in 12 of 39 felonies and sentenced to 28 years in federal prison. But in the intervening years Fonzo's son, first detained under Ciavarella as a teen for carrying drug paraphernalia, committed suicide.

age of twenty-three Her outcry carried a world of grief, and as she charged closer to the ex-judge the cameras found her, a stricken woman with blond hair and a face contorted in anger. "My kid's not *here*! He's *dead*! Because of *him*!" she wailed and pointed at Ciavarella. "You know what he told everybody in court? They need to be 'held accountable' for their *actions*! *You* need to be! Do you remember me? Do you remember me? Do you remember my *son*, an all-star wrestler? He's *gone*. He shot himself in the *heart*!"

Federal marshals found Fonzo and escorted her away while her bellowing continued in the background and cameras turned back to Ciavarella, who had remained impassive throughout Fonzo's outburst. A reporter finally asked him about her. "I don't know that lady," Ciavarella said. "I don't know what the facts and circumstances are concerning her son."

He reiterated what would become his trademark refrain: there had been no direct exchange of children for money. This was no kids for cash scheme.

---- CHAPTER 16 ----

FRISBEE, YOGA, SPIN

If the saga of Luzerne County can be chronicled in buildings—juvenile prisons, majestic courthouses, a luxury Florida condo—the aftermath, too, plays out in bricks and mortar. Federal prisons and two more houses in paradise lengthen the list.

In 2011 disgraced ex-judge Michael Conahan landed at the federal prison in Miami to begin serving his 17.5 year sentence. The low-security prison was built in 1976 for juvenile offenders and today houses about one thousand adult men. In June of 2020, halfway through his sentence and at the outset of the COVID-19 pandemic, Conahan made a bid for compassionate release. In a note written in his own hand, Conahan said he suffered from high blood pressure, heart issues, and Guillain-Barre syndrome, a rare disorder in which the immune system attacks the nerves. The set of ailments put him at "grave danger of not only contracting the virus, but of dying from the virus," he wrote. About ten days later, Conahan was released.

The dwelling that would serve for Conahan's house arrest was a waterfront condominium in The Estuary in Delray Beach, Florida, bought without a mortgage by his wife in 2011 for about $650,000, or more than $2 million in 2023 dollars. Barbara Conahan bought the largest-size model townhouse in the complex, the Vespucci, with three bedrooms, three baths, three stories, and 3,317 square feet.

As with every other bit of news on the judges, Conahan's release enraged some in Luzerne County, especially Sandy Fonzo. Fonzo knew the reasons for her son's suicide were complex and unknowable. But when, in 2020, Fonzo learned of Conahan's furlough and house arrest, she lashed out again.

"There is no reason [Conahan] couldn't be treated in the prison," Fonzo told a reporter. "They have medical staff there. The virus is spreading all over Florida. He'd probably be safer in prison. Instead, he gets to live in paradise while the rest of us struggle to get by. I just can't believe it."

○─○─○

Robert Powell served eighteen months in federal prison for failing to report the kids-for-cash scandal. The jury, apparently, did not believe he had been extorted by the judges. Disbarred, he lives now in a roughly $5 million mansion in the Frenchman's Reserve Country Club in Palm Beach Gardens—with six bedrooms, eight bathrooms, seventeen TVs, an elevator, an infinity pool, a spa, and views of a lake and golf course. Newspaper reports said he and his wife were also registered owners of a Maserati and a Mercedes-Benz worth a combined two hundred thousand dollars.

Gregory Zappala, Powell's ex-partner, claimed Powell had bilked him of millions of dollars. In court filings, Zappala painted a shady picture of Powell, alleging he had used an alias, formed a Cayman Islands company, taken "[duffel] bags of cash" to Costa Rica, and made "frequent trips to Switzerland." For his part, Powell argued that Zappala had treated his distress as an "opportunity." But those competing allegations were never tested in court because Zappala and Powell ended their lawsuits against each other in 2015 and never divulged the outcome.

Developer Robert Mericle served a year in federal prison, then returned to his thriving commercial real estate and construction company in northeastern Pennsylvania.

∞

A thousand miles north of Conahan's luxury place of house arrest, a compound of brick buildings sprawls across twenty-seven acres in northeastern Kentucky. Guard towers and concertina wire are features of the federal prison in Ashland, near the borders of Ohio and West Virginia. It is another low-security complex and was built in 1940 to house bootleggers and IRS violators.

Today Ashland is highly sought after for its low levels of violence. *Forbes Magazine* named it one of the ten cushiest prisons in the country. Among the most notable of its roughly 1,300 male inmates is Mark Ciavarella, whose release date is June 18, 2035, when he will be eighty-four.

Inmates at Ashland share double rooms, and available activities can sound like Leisure World, with classes in jazz, rock 'n' roll,

The federal prison at Ashland in eastern Kentucky, where Mark Ciavarella is serving his 28-year sentence, is a low-security prison favored by white-collar criminals for its low levels of violence.

and Japanese; training in welding and gardening; sports activities like baseball, tennis, and ultimate Frisbee; and exercise classes in spin and yoga. While at Ashland Ciavarella has, since 2011, filed numerous appeals and had some of his most serious convictions overturned, though he has been unable to shorten his twenty-eight-year-sentence.

In December of 2020 Ciavarella, too, sought a "compassionate release" from prison due to the COVID-19 pandemic, saying he suffered many medical ills, including chronic kidney disease. If exposed to the virus, his attorneys argued, Ciavarella might succumb.

By then a slew of civil actions against the two judges was playing out, revealing a vast and undertold victims' side of the

story. It wasn't lost on assistant US Attorney Mike Consiglio that while he prepared the government's response to Ciavarella's request, the same federal judge who would decide his fate was also presiding over civil hearings that graphically described the human consequences of Ciavarella's cruelty. "All I had to do was say, 'Your honor, as this court is probably aware, the long-term results of [Ciavarella's] criminal conduct still permeate the community,'" Consiglio said.

The Judge, Christopher C. Conner of the US District Court for the Middle District of Pennsylvania, ruled in June of 2022. Ciavarella "persists in downplaying the overall criminal scheme and his role within it," the judge wrote. He reiterated that

Ciavarella had committed "a massive breach of the public trust, causing harm to vulnerable juvenile victims and badly damaging the integrity of the state's judicial system. . . . This defendant knew better—or, at the very least, he should have."

He denied the request.

CHAPTER 17

UNIMAGINABLE BRUTALITY

In two high-ceilinged, wood-paneled federal courthouses in the fall of 2021, 313 witnesses in a class-action lawsuit, first filed more than a decade earlier, testified about their years lost or warped out of recognizable shape after Judge Mark Ciavarella sent them through the mysterious courtroom door and into the juvenile justice system. Now those children and youths were in their late twenties and early thirties, and they poured out their stories in anguished testimony, either in court or by video during the height of the COVID-19 pandemic.

In a radical departure from the toxic courtrooms run by

the cheating judges, Judge Christopher C. Conner, of the US District Court for the Middle District of Pennsylvania, listened to the victims' stories with grave calm, projecting a long-sought legal and moral authority, even as the plaintiffs testified from home offices, cluttered kitchens, hospital beds, cars, workplaces, and state prisons. They called from Florida, from California, and from the small towns around Luzerne County that they had never left.

Despite the random and sometimes private home settings, the hearings carried the weight of a truth and reconciliation commission, the kind that convenes to investigate war crimes. This was about young lives and whole families destroyed at the hands of the American legal system. Amid the classic columns, polished marble, and detailed woodworking of courtrooms in Harrisburg and Wilkes-Barre, the restrained, patrician-looking Conner reacted with frank horror as former juveniles and their parents poured out life stories in vivid words and pictures. Here was the aftermath, or what the federal judge later described as the vast human toll. The stealing and manipulating, the underground pathways of stolen millions, the punishments and appeals—all had been outlined and detailed. These plaintiffs recorded the legacy. It washed outward from the judges' crimes like the wake of a ship, waves still slamming and eroding the shoreline.

On one October day in Harrisburg, Judge Conner listened via Zoom to Rebecca Hackney as she recalled an order by Ciavarella during her 2004 hearing, the one where he asked her to count the number of buttons on her blouse.

Judge Conner leaned forward and tried to clarify. There had to have been more to Hackney's wrongdoing. He waited, then inquired.

"That's it?"

"That is it, yes," replied Hackney, a young mother in a pink fleece with long pink-painted fingernails who spoke to the court from her home in Seneca Falls, New York. A toddler zipped around behind her.

"Was there something else?" the judge asked, trying to make sense of her case.

"Absolutely not," Hackney replied.

"So the only thing you did was drive the wrong way down a one-way street?" the judge repeated, trying to understand.

"That is correct," said Hackney.

"I'm speechless," said the judge.

"So was my family," Hackney replied.

"I'm flabbergasted at the penalty imposed," he added.

There was more. A few days after she entered Pennsylvania Child Care, which mandated daily recreation, Hackney chose to play football rather than walk laps around a perimeter. During the game she was tackled by a larger young woman, and the full force of the other girl's weight plus her own landed on Hackney's elbow in the pileup. Hackney felt pieces of shattered bone moving in her elbow. The pain was unbearable, she said, but it took two days before the staff sent her for medical help. They handcuffed and shackled Hackney for her trip to a doctor, who inserted metal pins that remain to this day. "It affects the way I carry things," she said.

While in placement, Hackney also suffered the death of the grandmother who had raised her. She attended the funeral, grief-stricken, handcuffed, and shackled. "Being a child, having that be the starting point of my life . . ." she said. It was, in hindsight, the start of a depression that led to addiction. "Everything went downhill after that."

The slightly formal, white-haired Conner sought to find words. "Your situation is so far outside of reality for me," he said. "It's so far outside the realm of appropriate justice."

He added: "Your story is remarkable."

It is hard to imagine Hackney was lucky, but another plaintiff, locked up at age eleven, was denied the right to attend his mother's funeral after her death from cancer. "None of them would let me go to her funeral," he told Judge Conner. "It really took a toll on me."

The detailed spoken testimony also revealed the Darwinian struggles for survival in many different juvenile facilities. The plaintiffs spoke of sexual and physical assaults, and of lifelong physical and mental harms difficult for victims to describe and listeners to hear. Grown men in prison jumpsuits and chains wept in video calls as they drew direct lines from simple youth pranks to Ciavarella's courtroom to youth lockup to their present-day lives behind bars. "My situation now I would blame totally on that," one inmate told the judge via video. "I make my own decisions, of course, but being sent away, alone, had an effect on where my life has led."

Another young man, beaten while in detention, said that after he got home, "no one wanted to speak to me, not even my parents. I dropped out of school and felt like nobody could help me." He wiped away tears with cuffed hands. He had turned to drinking to dull emotional pain, which is what had landed him behind bars as an adult. A prison guard handed him a paper towel roll. "I feel like my life got nowhere," he said. His feet shackled, he shuffled out of the room and the video screen.

The physical injuries juveniles endured while locked up fill a thirty-two-page spreadsheet prepared by attorneys representing the civil class action. It is a grim catalog of brutality: broken bones, mangled body parts, a gang rape, a gangrenous toe, scabies, a flashlight beating, partial blindness, a sexually transmitted disease from a sexual assault, overmedication or terrible withdrawal from needed medication. "Beat up by staff, forced to eat bugs," one entry says. "Walked on ice in bare skin," says another. A third: "Bleeding from shackles, treated like an animal." And one more: "Held down for six hours once."

Judge Conner later added, in a written decision, that many youths were denied or received inadequate medical care for maladies that included "an asthma attack, a dental abscess, an eye infection, a concussion, or a sprained ankle." One contracted tuberculosis while at Pennsylvania Child Care and required hospitalization. Two young women suffered yeast and urinary tract infections because the detention center kept underwear in general circulation, forcing youths to wear undergarments others had worn.

In more recent years, the detention experience had manifested in profound psychological ills: depression, anxiety, post-traumatic stress disorder, and alcohol and drug addiction. And there were those who later died by suicide and drug overdoses. Those youths were represented by their parents.

The plaintiffs' lead attorney, Sol H. Weiss, who gained notoriety in a class action against the NFL related to player concussions, later said his legal team's strategy in the Kids for Cash case was to include each day two of the most "extraordinarily devastating stories" from among the three hundred-plus witnesses. All were affecting, he said, but a few stuck with him especially.

"One guy walked into the courtroom who was friendly with

Ciavarella," Weiss later told a reporter, "and he had [brought] a paper bag into the courtroom. In the bag were all sorts of things he had from his son. He said he turned in his son because the son was verbally fighting with [the boy's] mother, and because he knew Ciavarella and he thought Ciavarella would scare the daylights out of the kid—give him probation or something and that would end it.

"Ciavarella put the kid away," Weiss recalled. "The mother and father divorced after that, then the kid turned to drugs and suicide." His father, Weiss said, "was literally shaking and crying on the stand. I think he had the urn on the stand with his son's ashes."

Another case involved "a girl whose father was molesting and raping her. She reported that, but Ciavarella turned it around on her and said, 'How dare you try to put a good man behind bars?' and he put her away."

∞

The aggregated data from the class action reveal a story of innocence lost. Of the 275 former juveniles who testified in the civil case, seventy-eight youths—more than a quarter—were thirteen years old or younger when they went before Ciavarella. And they had been arrested for essentially being kids: thirty-three smoked marijuana or had paraphernalia; twenty-seven were caught up in school fights; twenty-two had fights at home; ten drank alcohol while underage; eight carried pocketknives; four smoked at school; five had unpaid small fines; one stole a Hershey Bar; and one peeled paint off the side of a school swimming pool.

One boy was so young that a slightly older girl, waiting her turn in Ciavarella's court, noticed. "I watched an eight-year-old boy sent away from his grandmother," Elizabeth Lorenz, now a graduate student, told Judge Conner from what appeared to be her kitchen table, where soft light from a nearby window poured through blinds. She wore glasses, her hair pulled back. "And I thought, 'Something is wrong.' I was looking around at all the adults in the room and wondering why no one was helping," she added.

Lorenz had a bright future ahead when she was caught, at fifteen, with three of her parents' opioid pain pills in her purse, meant for one of her teammates on the school basketball team. Ciavarella sentenced her to Pennsylvania Child Care for thirty-two days, followed by probation. Two years later her father found a single pain pill in her purse. She found herself, once again, in front of Ciavarella. Her parents begged Ciavarella for a shorter stay because she had a large college scholarship. "He said no," she said.

It had taken seven years to get her life back on track, she told the court. Now she wants to help other children and young adults do the same.

But others remain far off the track, and the lost dreams and opportunities at Ciavarella's and his co-conspirators' hands abound. At least two young men were unable to fulfill military service, even when one was accompanied to juvenile court by an army recruiter who vouched for the youth. Ciavarella was unmoved, and the young man lost a signing bonus and his hopes for that future, he told the federal judge. A "shockingly high number" can't find consistent employment, said attorney Weiss in his closing argument.

And families on the margins lost many thousands of dollars due to the extraordinary expenses associated with juvenile detention. Already, the families of the detained youths came from a generally more vulnerable, lower socio-economic class across Luzerne County, advocates later said. The astronomical fees associated with their child's detention did grave economic harm to some. One parent paid out about twenty-five thousand dollars in total for her son's detention, she told the court. Another young woman, jailed at thirteen after a school fight, said that her parents paid $4,400 for her release but then lost the family home. A young man testified that his father, the sole earner in the family, was charged three hundred dollars weekly for his son's detention and got behind. "My father lost his father's house as a result," he told Judge Conner. Another young man, detained at twelve and now thirty, testified that he was back on his feet with a job, an apartment, and a car. But his mother had drained her retirement fund to help him recover from addiction and poor mental health brought on by detention. The Jerock children remained on probation for two years while their mother, who sold corporate phone systems, and their father, who worked in a pizza parlor, scraped together the six thousand dollars in fees.

But one family with deeper pockets was able to obtain their son's release by paying five thousand dollars directly to Ciavarella, one witness said.

⌗⌗⌗

The educational legacy of the class action group reveals losses in social mobility and earning power. If elite families give their all to college preparation to ensure their children an economic and social leg up, Ciavarella delivered an educational smackdown. At least sixty-five youths who were part of the class action dropped out of high school. In the lawyers' spreadsheet of harms done, notations include: "Completed sixth grade" and "dropped out in the 7th grade" and "dropped out 8th grade" and "straight A student until 8th grade" and "lost all scholarship offers" and "lost scholarship to Temple University."

Many plaintiffs endured assaults of all kinds at facilities later investigated and shut down. In 2001, at age twelve, Ryan Lamoreaux was caught with some of his classmates vandalizing a school bathroom in Wilkes-Barre. When Judge Ciavarella, the sports lover, learned Lamoreaux played football, he told him: "You will graduate from Glen Mills [Schools]." Then a seventh-grader, Lamoreaux stood in court and counted out on his fingers the extraordinary sentence of five years of detention at this notorious reform school for boys outside Philadelphia, known then for its elite football team.

Twenty years later, at thirty-three, Lamoreaux stood before Judge Conner in the elegant federal courthouse in Wilkes-Barre. He was crisply dressed in a sweater and tie and wearing a closely trimmed beard over facial tattoos. It was the first time he had spoken publicly about his lost years at Glen Mills, which was shut down by the state in 2019 after the *Philadelphia Inquirer* exposed unspeakable sexual assaults and violence condoned and encouraged by staff. Lamoreaux had composed a victim impact statement, which he had thought he would read directly to the judges, though at this hearing, the disgraced men presented no defense.

"Have you ever felt you had to live a gladiator lifestyle just to literally breathe another day?" Lamoreaux read to the court in October of 2021. "Have you ever experienced being physically/sexually assaulted, legitimately choked unconscious, kicked and punched in the face . . . ?"

Had they ever watched a child being sexually assaulted? Had they ever awakened in the middle of the night to someone sexually assaulting them? Had they ever been groomed to be a victim by someone they had thought they could trust?

Lamoreaux had, he told the court.

Finished with his two-page statement, Lamoreaux looked up,

his face wet. It was a strange feeling, to cry. He'd pushed away the pain of those five years until now. He glanced at his wife and his mother, both weeping in the courtroom. They were hearing details for the first time. He noticed the court stenographer gazing up at him and holding a tissue to her face. It looked to him like the whole courtroom was crying.

∞

Lamoreaux today appears to have transcended the harm done at Glen Mills, where, confusingly, Judge Ciavarella attended some of his football games and then his graduation. He manages a successful life as a federal employee with the US Postal Service, processing passports. He is grateful for a good salary, a loving wife, and four children. News of his emotional reading appeared in the local newspaper along with his photograph, leading to many words of support from customers, friends, and family.

But Lamoreaux's inner life is one of torment. He manages severe anxiety with medication. He wrestles with self blame though he knows it is irrational. He flashes back to the times he was victimized—and to his victimization of others, for which he feels terrible guilt, though he knows that at gladiatorial Glen Mills he had only two choices, victim or victimizer. He, like many others, sees how his past has taken a toll on his family. Often frustrated or angry parents were the ones to contact police, hoping the call alone, or a light consequence, might deter bad behavior. Now, many years later, some grown children still feel betrayed by those calls, while parents carry an anvil of guilt on their backs. Repair comes slowly if at all.

Lamoreaux in turn worries about his parenting

"The way I parent sometimes is like a counselor at [Glen

Mills], more like a drill instructor than a parent," Lamoreaux said. "Then I take a step back, I see how my traumas from years ago surface and then trickle down to my children. And I think how will that affect my kids in 20 years? It's generational trauma."

Lamoreaux didn't know what to do with his victim impact statement. Throw it away? Delete from his files? He decided to lock it up in his personal safe. It was there if he wanted to be reminded, but hidden away for now as he lived his life. And he didn't care much about hitting some cash jackpot from the class-action case. The meaning for him had come from being heard.

"You had to get it out," Lamoreaux reflected. "People needed to know more than that kids were sitting in jail cells for 12 or 24 months. The abuse, the assaults—our mental health as a whole—it was completely overlooked when we were sentenced, and the impact of our sentences wasn't considered."

The testimony of so many had revealed the brutality of men in power without conscience. "It's like all morality left their bodies for a dollar sign," he said.

But in airing that ugly and tragic chapter he had found relief from an extremely unlikely place: a judge in a courtroom.

CHAPTER 18

HARM
REDUCTION

On a Tuesday afternoon in June of 2022, a group of teenagers from Newark, New Jersey, pop up one-by-one on a video call as participants in a different kind of juvenile court, one that has former youth offenders deciding the fate of new youth offenders in what is called youth court. On this day a young man, W., whose virtual background is a courtroom, will preside as the judge of this Newark Youth Court hearing, held via Zoom during the COVID-19 pandemic. He is joined by teens who will assume courtroom roles—as bailiff, foreperson (of the jury), community advocate (prosecutor), youth advocate (defense attorney), jurors, and respondent (defendant).

The bailiff introduces Judge W., who administers an oath of confidentiality to the group. The bailiff swears in the respondent, E., an eighth grader from a Newark public school. She has been accused of assaulting another girl in an incident that took place earlier in the year at a McDonald's. Her case was diverted from normal courtroom channels to this youth court hearing.

The community advocate begins by noting that violence harms a community and can easily escalate. E. could have been critically hurt if the victim and her friends had retaliated. And assault is a serious offense. If E. were convicted of assault it would stain her record and likely harm her future

Then the youth advocate speaks up for E., a funny and cheerful fourteen-year-old who loves dance and is passionate about basketball. E. is responsible about her schoolwork. While not an A student, E. keeps track of her assignments and grades and checks in with her teachers.

GᴓᴓᴓƆ

Judge W. asks, "E., do you have anything you'd like to say on your own behalf at this time?"

Yes, E. says: "I have had a conversation with the girl and apologized to her for everything. I don't even know what came over me, honestly. I think it was peer pressure. I'm not friends with that group anymore. I have completely walked away."

Others ask E. questions. Can she describe what happened?

"I went to McDonald's and my friends went to McDonald's and then this girl entered the building and my friends said, 'Let's just hit her; let's hit her; let's get her.' They just kept going and going like that. Until we hit her."

"Do you consider yourself a follower or a leader?"

"At that time I was a follower," E. says. "I'm usually a leader."

Did E. have any future goals in mind?

"I really, really hope to get into college," she says, "especially with a basketball scholarship. I really, really love writing." She is interested in studying business, too.

"Do you also know that this action can affect your future goals?"

"I do know that and I really, really regret it," E. says.

"What was going through your mind at that moment when your friends told you to hit the girl?"

"Worriedness."

"Why didn't you walk away?"

"I don't even know why I didn't walk away, honestly. I just feel like I did it because they were the cool kids and I wanted to fit in with them, but honestly I regret it."

"How do you feel about being here today?"

"Disappointed in myself." Her parents are upset, too.

"What do you think you should take away from this situation?"

"Not following others," E. says.

There are closing statements and then, in a breakout room, the jury deliberates. E. has taken responsibility. She has apologized to the victim. She has understood the negative consequences of her actions to herself and others. And she has taken steps to change— by distancing herself from the group under whose influence she struck the girl.

The jurors arrive at a set of sanctions, which they share with the group. E. will be required to participate in two sessions of community service. She must take a skill-building workshop on decision making and another on conflict resolution. She will need at least one session with a social worker, who will help E. connect with support services like psychological counseling and a youth basketball program.

Under these conditions, if completed, E. will face no detention and will have no juvenile record.

ᖍᖎᖏ

The Newark Youth Court, launched in 2008, illustrates the latest in juvenile justice. An abundance of research has pulled the curtain on detention for first-time, low-level offenders: it ruins lives and costs millions. While Ciavarella filled detention centers, the rest of the country, from California to Maine, was taking drastic action to close them. About half have shut down over nearly two decades, according to federal data: from 3,047 in 2000 to 1,510 in 2018. And the number of youths detained in the US has also dropped radically—by 77 percent over twenty years—from 108,802 youths in placement in 2000 to 25,014 in 2020, according to the Office of Juvenile Justice and Delinquency Prevention. The number of youth courts, on the other hand, also known as teen courts or peer courts, has multiplied—to more than 1,400 across the US. In these courts, low-level juvenile offenders are prosecuted, defended, and sentenced by their peers.

"The research tells us that delinquent behavior is normal adolescent behavior," explains Liz Ryan, administrator for the office at the US Department of Justice and the top US official for jailed kids. She has led a crusade to shut down detention centers across the country. "Most young people will engage in delinquent behavior during their teenage years. And the good news is that most young people will age out of that delinquent behavior as they mature."

Newark's youth court was begun by former Chief Municipal Judge Victoria Pratt with an assist from US Senator (and former Newark mayor) Cory Booker. It is one among at least thirty in the country that employs procedural justice, named for an emphasis on how people are treated—or the fine-grained interactions between people and the law at every stage of the legal process. Procedural justice emphasizes fairness from a person's first contact with a police officer to a visit with a probation officer to the back-and-forth interactions with a judge in a courtroom. The quality of each of these interactions can have a profound effect on outcomes, research has shown. An evangelist for the method, Judge Pratt had grown tired of the revolving door of her courtroom, which she likened in a TED Talk to a reserved seat in a tragic reality show with no ending. She details the creation of the alternative court process in her 2022 book, *The Power of Dignity.*

She points to research on procedural justice, which shows that if young people experience the court as fair, and are treated with dignity and respect, they tend to follow the law, even when a judge rules against them. Adding to those findings is the landmark "Crossroads in Juvenile Justice" study, published in 2020 by Cambridge University Press. That five-year study of 1,200 youths from three US cities, led by University of California, Irvine, professor Elizabeth Cauffman, found that formal juvenile detention does more harm than good across dozens of measures: in a youth's education, employment, emotional maturity, drug use, impulse control, callousness, and criminal behavior. It concludes that informal detention, which instead of confining youths requires them to perform community service, can achieve the twin goals of public safety and rehabilitation.

∞

"When people are incarcerated very bad things happen, lots of bad things happen," said Cauffman, noting that youths who are locked up drop out of civic life, losing access to both schooling and work, the pillars of a successful adulthood. "Your life is completely disrupted."

People need to be held accountable for wrongdoing, Cauffman insists, but with methods that work. In 2018 she helped launch the Young Adult Court in Orange County, California, to treat first-time, nonviolent felony offenders. The two-year program provides counseling, job training, addiction treatment, and help with housing and transportation to eighteen-to-twenty-three-year-olds. One of the first graduates, Thomas (his first name) was facing nine years in prison after committing a robbery. He spent eighteen months meeting weekly with youth court staff.

In January of 2021, Thomas wore a charcoal-colored suit and oxford shirt to his graduation in Orange County Superior Court, where he addressed Judge Maria Hernandez. "I apologize to the people I hurt in the process of my wrongdoings," he said. "This court has helped me—a Black man—have a second chance at life instead of throwing me into jail. I was given an opportunity to redeem myself. Now, I have a job in dermatology and plastic surgery and I make good money. I was able to buy a car and have the opportunity for more growth." The felony offense would be stricken from his record. Via Zoom in midpandemic, court staff, family, friends, and others of the twenty-five young adult participants enrolled with Thomas cheered him in his moment.

⬤⬤⬤

That outcome veered drastically from those that played out weekly at the Luzerne County Juvenile Court during the scandal-plagued years. The injurious outcomes under the judges tend to prove the truth of the Crossroads study in a different way. Treating children and youths with contempt; delivering capricious and harsh sentences for the smallest offenses; offering no support for youths trying to recover from whatever led to their misbehavior—all of these methods promise poor outcomes.

It is hard to imagine how life might have turned out differently for Carisa Tomkiel if she and her best friend, Angelia, had been brought before a youth court for their sign scribbling in West Pittston. For the past eighteen years Tomkiel has struggled to separate herself from the effects of juvenile court, detention, probation with house arrest, and widespread school and community shunning. In her small town it can be hard to ignore the harsh gaze of others, first encountered during her high school years. But a caring partner, supportive family, years of therapy, and testifying in federal court have all somehow served to loosen the death grip of self-loathing that had kept Carisa depressed and unengaged for nearly two decades.

"I know other kids had it way worse than I did," she said, "but you can't really judge how somebody's going to take something mentally. I'm obviously one of the unlucky ones in that it kind of broke my brain. But I'm also at that point where I'm not going to let [Ciavarella] ruin my life any more than he already did. If I do then he wins. It's kind of time to move on."

Recently Carisa decided to get a driver's license. With her partner's coaxing, she enrolled in a driving school and spent two hours parallel parking to achieve mastery. Now, at thirty-two, Carisa has her license. She and her partner went out for pizza to celebrate. "I'm kind of ready to do my own thing," she said. "I don't want to be on disability because of having a broken brain."

She is considering a return to school and a career in mental health advocacy or even nursing. She doesn't know how or exactly where. She trusts one thing and it might seem small to others but not to her. "I know I'm on track to have everything stay on track."

CHAPTER 19

BRANDED

Matthew Samson's story encapsulates the long-term brokenness caused by juvenile detention. In 2007 Samson was a scrawny, blond ten-year-old who raced his collection of miniature stock cars down the neighborhood slide. He hadn't understood the gravity of his actions that summer night in Luzerne, a small town north of Wilkes-Barre. When an older friend persuaded him to climb through an open window at Frank's Market in the neighborhood, then unlock the door from inside, Matthew hadn't thought "break-in" or "robbery." He didn't know the legal meaning of the words. His friend had lured him with the promise of a Hot Wheels car. Matthew took two and a bag of potato chips. He couldn't wait to send the two new cars whooshing down the slide. He would pay Frank back later. But then his older

Matthew Samson was an especially small child of ten when he was tapped by an older friend to crawl through a window to rob a neighborhood grocery. The boys were caught, and Samson was judged delinquent and sent to a wilderness camp on weekends and a vocational program after school. The experience taught Samson how to be a criminal, he says, and today he struggles against an identity that defines not him but rather the judge who sentenced him.

friend ransacked the cash register, where he found a key to the vending machine outside. His friend opened the machine and pushed a button and the cash box began spewing coins like a slot machine. "What are we doing?" asked Matthew. "We came here for toys." By then Matthew didn't know how to stop his friend or get away.

The police caught the boys, and soon they stood before Judge Mark Ciavarella, who sat up high on his elevated bench looking down. Matthew looked around the courthouse to see the older kids in orange jumpsuits and shackles. He was one third their size and petrified, and he would never forget that judge's face, stony and blank. The judge sentenced Matthew to house arrest for six months, with weekends at a wilderness boot camp, and weekday afternoons at a vocational school, creating a kind of wraparound-exposure to teenagers who stole cars, sold drugs, and had no use for school or work. A police officer took Matthew's fingerprints and fastened a monitor too tightly around his ankle. It felt to Matthew like a certification—of his status as a criminal.

And with a click of that monitor, Matthew Samson's life jumped the track. After school, his classmates climbed onto their yellow school buses while Matthew disappeared into a large white van with an identifying logo on the side. He tried to wait until other kids had left, but everyone saw him board the bus to the bad-kids after-school program. There he took in new words and concepts, like using or selling marijuana, speed, or Adderall. That was confusing. He was taking Adderall. "Why would *they* take that?" Matthew wondered to himself. "*I* take that and I don't like the way it makes me feel. It makes me feel calm, like I'm not myself."

Within minutes of arriving at the wilderness camp, a veteran instructor called Matthew aside. "What the heck did you *do?*" he asked Matthew, who drew attention from all corners of the camp for his size and age. Many told him he didn't belong there. The counselor tried to look out for Matthew. But the older kids saw a blank canvas. They told him to forget all sorts of life rules, like doing homework, going to school, or getting a job.

Back at school, people decided Matthew was a criminal. He acquired a nickname, Bad Matthew, which burrowed under his skin. The school principal, a jokester, called out in the hallway, "Hey, Bad Matthew, am I going to see you in my office again today?" His former friends and neighbors shunned him. Shopkeepers tracked him in their stores. Adult siblings called him a black sheep, predicted prison before eighteen, and banned him from family gatherings—and from seeing his beloved younger nephew. In no time, Matthew Samson came to see his toy car and potato chip theft not as a ten-year-old-boy mistake, but as proof that he was born bad and would die bad.

"Everyone says I'm bad so I must be bad," he said to himself.

●○●

A few who testified in the federal courtrooms in the fall of 2021 reported to Judge Christopher C. Conner that they had moved on with their lives. One is a stockbroker, another a teacher and writer; others have advanced degrees. "Thank *God* I met somebody who loved me enough to let me learn to love myself," said Stephanie Romanski, who testified via Zoom while driving the streets of greater Miami wearing a sky-blue polo shirt bearing her company's insignia, "Pool Care Miami."

"Ciavarella didn't ruin all of me," she added.

Sober for more than five years, Romanski credits her strong relationship with her partner for her recovery, not to mention her large garden of exotic orchids and her menagerie of animals, including two talking birds who regularly whistle and squawk, "I [expletive] *love* you!"

But in his 2022 written opinion in the class action, Judge Conner, of the US District Court of the Middle District of Pennsylvania, addressed one especially insidious harm among others: the "emotional and reputational damages post-detention."

Like Matthew Samson, many who returned to their communities endured devastating public rejection. Their stories called to mind Nathaniel Hawthorne's *The Scarlet Letter*, in which a young woman, Hester Prynne, who has an adulterous affair and gives birth to a daughter, is publicly condemned by Puritan townspeople for the rest of her life.

"Their reputation was damaged by virtue of being labeled a 'bad kid,'" Judge Conner said in his closing comments in court. "I can't think of anything more difficult to overcome in middle school or high school. The impact on social interactions, the treatment by people in the community. That harm is far-reaching."

After detention, one young man was escorted by a security guard to every high school class, Conner noted. Another, originally arrested at school, fought off waves of anxiety when he returned. "I was labeled," he told Judge Conner. Carisa Tomkiel, accused of graffiti spraying in West Pittston, was mortified when back at high school the phone would ring in a classroom and it was the probation lady, summoning her from class for drug testing. Everyone knew she then had to urinate into a cup and carry the sample through the halls from the restroom back to the probation office, though her case was unrelated to drugs. It felt like a walk of shame.

"The backlash was crazy," Tomkiel recalled. "We didn't get any support from anybody. The people around us believed everything that was being said. We were just bad kids, bad influences, on the road to nowhere."

Tomkiel and her best friend, Angelia, ate lunch alone every day in the cafeteria. Tomkiel grew to hate her school, her classmates, her teachers. "Kids don't forget," she said. "They're cruel. Even now I can't stand seeing a group of teenagers laughing because in my head it just makes me think about the past."

A majority who testified were rejected by old friends whose parents banned the "delinquent" from their homes and warned their own children to stay away. Even teachers and coaches shunned returning youths. "Coaches didn't want a criminal on their team," one man said in court. He gave up sports.

After April Jerock and her brother were detained for a month for entering the abandoned house, they were locked out of their friend group and treated "like little gangsters," April said. "We were the running joke for at least two years." At school, the children were both pulled from class for drug testing. Robert, with a learning impairment, was mocked by classmates who followed him around and sang a pop song, "Locked Up." The feeling of red-hot shame visited their parents, too. "They were garnishing our wages," said Deborah Jerock. "That was embarrassing. Right away your employer knew there was something."

<hr>

On August 16 of 2022, Judge Conner rendered an impassioned written decision in the class action. "Although most memories fade over the years," Judge Conner wrote, "certain events are so punctuated by overwhelming circumstances and emotions that no amount of time can erase their mark." The collective testimony of the 313 plaintiffs, he said, paints a "portrait of justice derailed by a presiding judge who ruled with breathtaking arrogance and an unfathomable disregard of due process."

The ruling was forwarded by attorneys to the 313 plaintiffs, and one sentence in the forty pages leapt out for many: "The court finds the victims' testimony to be completely credible and credits their remembrances of specific events as well as their candid inability to remember others."

The federal judge summarized the defendants as "the tragic human casualties of a scandal of epic proportions."

"The law is powerless to restore to plaintiffs the weeks, months, and years lost because of the actions of the defendants. But we hope that by listening to their experiences and acknowledging the depth of the damage done to their lives, we can provide them with a measure of closure and, with this memorandum opinion, ensure that their stories are never forgotten."

The award, of punitive and compensatory damages, was for $206 million.

It was a strong message but hardly compensatory. The convicted judges, having liquidated their luxury assets, today have few or no assets—or none within reach of the court. Likely there would be no payout, though that was unsurprising to Ryan Lamoreaux. What mattered more was that he had told his story out loud, and that Judge Conner had listened and affirmed his credibility. The judge believed him.

"If I could take anything from this whole thing it'd be about Judge Conner," he said. "What he said meant more than any monetary compensation could. It was almost like an understanding. He understood. He felt for us. That made me feel better than a [dollar] number with commas ever could."

ↄ⊖ↄ

Over coffee in downtown Wilkes-Barre one day after the hearings, Matthew Samson described his post-detention life. "You get branded," said Samson, who is now twenty-four and wears his long brown hair pulled straight back. "It does something to your brain. You almost believe you're this bad person and you've gotta hang around these bad people. The people I started hanging out with were all just bad kids. They weren't nice people. After that I kind of lost my childhood. At thirteen, I was hanging around with drug dealers at trap houses, seeing things I shouldn't see in my whole life."

Samson dropped out of tenth grade, grew angry, then depressed and anxious. He gained weight. He developed paranoia. A few years ago he met a woman who helped pull him away from the unsavory people he had known. Together they have a son, Noah, who is "absolutely brilliant and a perfect bundle of joy," Matthew says.

"He's just an amazing, amazing kid," Matthew boasts while sharing cell phone snapshots. "Everybody says he is the smartest kid they've ever met, even the doctor. I don't know how I got such a smart kid."

Noah, at two, could read words. Noah learned I Spy in five minutes. Noah already has a college fund. Noah smiles when Matthew walks in the door or when he and his dad take naps together. "He'll lie in bed next to me and say, 'Daddy sleeping, Daddy night, night,'" says Matthew. "He's definitely my rock."

Half his family still won't speak to Matthew Samson. He is unemployed and applying for social security to compensate for his poor mental health. He is also an old soul. He thinks about labels like good and bad—labels toxic to a kid's sense of self. He sees now what actually happened. He wasn't born bad, and he won't die bad. He made an ordinary childish mistake and a couple of corrupt judges took advantage. Who, exactly, was "bad" in Matthew Samson's story? What was the definition of evil?

AUTHOR'S
NOTE

One April afternoon in 2022, I grabbed an ill-fitting hard hat from a boxful near the entrance to the Lackawanna Coal Mine in Scranton, Pennsylvania, feeling like an overgrown kid on a field trip. Northeastern Pennsylvania was new to me, as was the life of a coal miner, so I thought a trip into black hell, as miners called it, might help me to understand.

Soon my group of a dozen or so would-be miners ducked into a noisy metal car attached to a cable, and we began our angled descent into a cave I couldn't quite see. I don't love enclosures, so I kept my eye on the sunny trapezoid shape of the mine entrance as it grew smaller and smaller until any ray of light vanished behind us. I wondered when the last time this shuttered mine, opened in 1860 and closed in 1966, had been inspected. Were we safe as visitors?

Our guide's lively narration helped me to focus on the related facts of mining life. But by then I perhaps knew too much—about the explosions, fires, floods, collapses, asphyxiations, and runaway coal cars that had killed or injured many thousands of miners over decades. I looked down the dark slope, lit now by electrical lights, and tried to imagine being lowered into this sunless place every day, knowing all the ways one could die.

This visit to a coal mine was, on the one hand, years and miles away from the court scandal I was writing about. And yet the more research I did for *Shackled*, the more I saw what I have seen before: that the history of a place defines the place, that history repeats itself, that past is prologue, that all of those adages about history offering breadcrumbs to the present applied here. The culture and dynamics of coal mining had found its way into a courthouse in Luzerne County.

The field trip was in some ways the fault of my editor, Susan Dobinick, who had a good hunch, I imagine, when she sent me a link to a documentary, *Kids for Cash*, released in 2013 and directed by Robert May. She happened to have grown up in the region and was familiar with the story. She also knew, from our work together on a previous project, that I had an interest in writing about injustice, especially when it involves children and young adults. The movie included interviews with several child victims and their families as well as lengthy interviews with the two judges before they pled and were found guilty. Watching it, I felt aghast, angry, distraught—that grown men could harm their community's children in order to get rich quick. The story was dark and disturbing, and Susan suggested that if I wanted to take on the project, I had better get a puppy to protect my mental health. Our household wound up with two.

When authors and journalists gather material for their stories they try to get as close to the facts and feeling of a story as possible. They get physically close to where stories take place; they try peering into the minds and memories of the people they are writing about; and they scour the written record until there is nothing left to see. The very best of them go to ridiculous lengths to get close, like Nellie Bly, one of the first American women journalists who checked herself into an insane asylum in 1887 to document horrific treatment of patients there. Robert Caro, a modern-day biographer of President Lyndon Johnson, hauled buckets of water from a deep well in the Texas hill country and then carried them on a yoke across his back from the well to the nearby farmhouse—in order to understand one facet of Johnson's grueling early years. Other authors and journalists have lived in the slums of Mumbai, worked as prison guards, taken minimum wage jobs, jumped trains, climbed Everest, lived in cars to write about nomadic Americans, and imbedded themselves with military units to write about wars around the world. Many, of course, have perished on the job.

I didn't carry a pickax, nor did I blast or chisel coal from the Lackawanna Mine in Scranton that day, nor have I spent time in detention, though my late parents may have thought that a good idea once. But I did stop in at the county's shuttered juvenile detention center, known as Pennsylvania Child Care, where I walked around the razor-wired property, peered into opaque windows, and snooped through the thick doors of the front lobby, where a notable Zero Tolerance poster was still stuck to the wall. I visited the majestic county courthouse and the less majestic courthouse annex in downtown Wilkes-Barre and found the modern courtroom on an upper floor where the disgraced county judge, Mark Ciavarella, sentenced many of the six thousand children and youth throughout the late 1990s and early 2000s. I had lunch at Perkins, the pancake house, where another corrupt judge, Michael Conahan, and a mob boss hatched schemes over their early morning omelets a few times a week. I also visited with some of Ciavarella's child victims, toured their old towns, visited their childhood homes, met with their parents, and was shown the scenes of their so-called crimes.

But in writing *Shackled* I relied more often on the vast written, video, and audio records about the case. This included an immense number of newspaper accounts, radio and TV reports, the documentary, many books and scholarly writings, and voluminous court filings. There were state hearings held soon after the case broke and available on videotape and in transcripts, and more recent hearings in a civil class action, which were open to the public. A podcast was recently released.

I consulted many books. The history of the Knox Mine Disaster has been well documented by Robert P., Kenneth C., and Nicole H. Wolensky in their book, *The Knox Mine Disaster*. The authors also wrote a companion book, *Voices of the Knox Mine Disaster*, which includes verbatim interviews with survivors, along with photographs of victims, survivors, and families. Robert Wolensky also directed me to his more recent book, co-authored with William A. Sr. Hastie, *Anthracite Labor Wars: Tenancy, Italians, and Organized Crime in the Northern Coalfield of Northeastern Pennsylvania 1897–1959*.

In addition, Paul A. Shackel's book, *Remembering Lattimer*, describes the violence of that deadly day as well as the racial struggles and migration patterns that led to tensions in the region. A children's book, *Growing Up in Coal Country*, by Susan Campbell Bartoletti, tells the grueling story of child labor in the mines. Another academic book, *The Face of Decline*, by Thomas Dublin and Walter Licht, about the anthracite region during coal's heyday and after, also served as an important background source. A 1901 textbook written by Peter Roberts, *The Anthracite Coal Industry*, offered rich detail about the dangers of mining and the after-effects of mining accidents on communities.

Especially eye-opening were the histories of organized crime in the region, including, *The Quiet Don: The Untold Story of Mafia Kingpin Russell Bufalino*, written by a reporter from the region, Matt Birkbeck. In 2023, Birkbeck followed with *The Life We Chose: William "Big Billy" D'Elia and the Last Secrets of America's Most Powerful Mafia Family*. D'Elia was the adopted son of Russell Bufalino and heir to the Bufalino crime family—and a close lifelong friend of disgraced Judge Michael Conahan. Another organized crime book, *I Heard You Paint Houses*, by Charles Brandt, which was the inspiration for the movie *The Irishman*, tells an adjacent though overlapping story about organized crime throughout Pennsylvania. Other details about organized crime and the roles of Bufalino and D'Elia are also verified in both state and federal reports on organized crime in Pennsylvania.

The former chief judge of the Newark Municipal Court, Victoria Pratt, happens to live in my town and has written about the transformative power of restorative justice among children and youth in her 2022 book, *The Power of Dignity*. Judge Pratt, who established the alternative Newark Youth Court with the help of then-Mayor and now Senator Cory Booker, also led me to sit in on a Zoom session of youth court in Newark during the pandemic.

The book I consulted most as a guide to the scandal was William Ecenbarger's detailed *Kids for Cash*, published in 2012 and chronicling the case up through the criminal proceedings and the state investigative hearings that led to recommendations for reform. Ecenbarger's comprehensive account included interviews with some key sources who have since died, including Judge Chester Muroski, who tried blowing the whistle only to be swiftly demoted. If newspapers write the first draft of history, Ecenbarger wrote the very compelling second one.

A Pulitzer-Prize-winning reporter, formerly of the *Philadelphia Inquirer*, Ecenbarger undoubtedly digested the hundreds of stories written by local and regional reporters and writers from the *Citizens' Voice* and the *Times Leader* newspapers in Wilkes-Barre; the *Times-Tribune* of Scranton; the *Standard-Speaker* of Hazleton; the *Legal Intelligencer* of Philadelphia; and the *Philadelphia Inquirer*, among others. Those many stories were written by reporters Craig R. McCoy, Terrie Morgan-Besecker, Mark Guydish, Dave Janoski, Michael Sisak, Jennifer Learn-Andes, and Michael P. Buffer, among many others. Reporters Leo Strupczewski, Zack Needles, Hank Grezlak, and Ben Present for the Philadelphia-based *Legal Intelligencer* also did groundbreaking work.

A former newspaper reporter myself, I can't help but point to the body of work produced by these reporters as a case study in local news reporting protecting democracy—at a time when America's local news system is collapsing. Local news reporting curbs corruption, lowers taxes, and allows people to feel more connected and less divided, many studies show. In Wilkes-Barre, local reporting led a state auditor to launch an immediate audit; led parents to come forward upon learning of others similarly situated; and revealed many connections that helped the FBI close in, finally, on the judges.

My reporting for *Shackled* started nearly two decades after the story's beginnings, and the more longitudinal look back allowed for a different view—at the altered life paths of the children and youths caught in the scandal. The elapsed time meant children and youth had acquired adult perspectives. It meant civil cases, held up during criminal proceedings, had wound through the courts to reveal more of the human costs. A new federal judge, Christopher C. Conner, took a more open approach to court filings and hearings related to the case than his predecessor. Time had enlarged the body of research that repudiates zero tolerance and the practice of detaining children and youths who have not committed violent crimes. And experiments in procedural justice, including the youth courts in Newark and in Orange County, California, have proven their value.

Throughout my records searches I developed a list of people who might talk with me directly, and I tracked some down via phone and social media. Some people wanted only to forget. Others had begun to shake off the guilt, shame, or anger of those earlier years. They were ready to talk.

That's how I found Carisa Tomkiel, who was at first reluctant. But her talking, she has said, including her testimony before Judge Conner in October of 2021, has helped her to take some steps forward that are meaningful to her, such as getting a driver's license and considering a career. Matthew Samson, too, has shed much of his "Bad Matthew" skin. He showed me the former convenience store and the back window where his older friend had pushed him through with the promise of a Hot Wheels car. Ryan Lamoreaux, whom I met outside of the Wilkes-Barre federal courthouse after closing arguments in the civil case, bravely shared with me a copy of his statement to the court, which he then locked up in his home safe.

I admired the documentary filmmakers' interviews with the two judges in *Kids for Cash*, which occurred after they had pled to the original charges but before the deal was scratched and new charges filed. I would have liked to include fresh material from them—to probe their psyches or even hear them repeat what they had already told others. Does Ciavarella still say he was acting in the best interests of children? Is it a hardship for Conahan to be on home confinement at his wife's luxury villa in Delray Beach? I was not surprised when their respective lawyers said the two men would not be interviewed for *Shackled*.

I never feel I have done enough research on any project, in part out of fear of missing some revelatory bit of the story that will make sense of it all. Inevitably, though, I arrive at the moments of getting organized and then, finally, writing.

I have tried many different methods of organizing, from writing a detailed outline or table of contents to highlighting, numbering and indexing every one of my notes and documents. I have used white boards, index cards, and Post-it notes. I have made drawings of rising action. I have subscribed to software designed especially to help writers get organized. The main help of any of these methods, I have found, is that each adds to a kind of osmosis of material.

By then my work space may look to an outsider like a hoarder's, with many piles of books, documents, reporters' notebooks, and index cards arranged on every surface. These piles, though, make rough sense to me. They are arranged in a chronology, and chronology becomes my organizing principle, along with the formulation of an overarching theme or idea that acts as a sword to cut away unrelated material. Friend and novelist Katherine Seligman notes that in fiction writing there are plotters and "pantsers," or those who construct their plot before they write and those who feel their way through a story by the seat of their pants. Pantsing is harder in nonfiction, but if you are predisposed to pantsing, as I am, then pantsing is how you must go.

One challenge in telling this story was in learning the very specific rules of county government, the proper functions of juvenile court, the correct roles of the many legal actors, from probation officers to police, public defenders, and district attorneys, as well as the many state and federal laws and regulations that shape a properly working juvenile justice system. To write about what's wrong you have to know how it is supposed to work correctly. Understanding the details, though, did not mean adding all of them to the story. On the other hand, the story required just enough detail to show what the crooks were doing wrong. Such refinements, of adding here, subtracting there, came with a bit of distance from the story, with copious rewriting, and finally and at many steps, with clear-eyed editing.

Once deep down in the Lackawanna Mine on that day in 2022 our guide thought it would be instructive to simulate total darkness. We all shut off our electronics. She hit the light switch. And there we stood, murmuring, chuckling uncomfortably, lifting our hands to within inches of our eyes to see what we could see. Nothing, it turned out. Absolutely nothing. A recreation of black hell in the middle of a lovely spring afternoon. I couldn't wait to get out.

SOURCE NOTES

CHAPTER 1 — PORTAL TO CALAMITY

"Just silly things.": Pennsylvania Interbranch Commission on Juvenile Justice. (December 7, 2009) "A.K." and "R.K." interviewed by Tod C. Allen. Transcript, p. 367. pacourts.us/Storage/media/pdfs/20210208/162530-dec7,2009.pdf.

"Very childish things . . . nothing gang-like.": Pennsylvania Interbranch Commission (December 7, 2009), p. 366. pacourts.us/Storage/media/pdfs/20210208/162530-dec7,2009.pdf.

"Shut up.": (quoting Judge Mark Ciavarella) Andrea Tomkiel, interview with author. March 22, 2021.

"You sit down . . . shut up.": Federal District Judge Christopher C. Conner decision, Wallace v. Powell, (August 16, 2022), p. 12. pamd.uscourts.gov/sites/pamd/files/opinions/09v286.pdf.

"What makes you think . . . crap?": Pennsylvania Interbranch Commission on Juvenile Justice. (April 1, 2010) Judge John C. Uhler asks Laurene Transue about her daughter, Hillary. Transcript, p. 29. pacourts.us/Storage/media/pdfs/20210208/162446-april1,2010.pdf.

"Zip, zip. That was it.": Pennsylvania Interbranch Commission on Juvenile Justice. (Nov. 9, 2009) Sandra Brulo interviewed by Judge Dwayne D. Woodruff. Transcript, pp. 231–232. pacourts.us/Storage/media/pdfs/20210208/162550-nov9,2009.pdf

"antics.": Pennsylvania Interbranch Commission (Nov. 9, 2009), p. 186. pacourts.us/Storage/media/pdfs/20210208/162550-nov9,2009.pdf.

"And then in the next breath . . . concern about that.": Pennsylvania Interbranch Commission (Nov. 9, 2009), p. 186. pacourts.us/Storage/media/pdfs/20210208/162550-nov9,2009.pdf.

"He let me go . . . feeling nice, he said.": Conner decision, Wallace v. Powell, p. 13. pamd.uscourts.gov/sites/pamd/files/opinions/09v286.pdf.

"R.K." "such a crazy case.": Pennsylvania Interbranch Commission (December 7, 2009), p. 369. pacourts.us/Storage/media/pdfs/20210208/162530-dec7,2009.pdf.

"The officer had told us . . . if Penn State loses.": Pennsylvania Interbranch Commission (December 7, 2009), p. 369. pacourts.us/Storage/media/pdfs/20210208/162530-dec7,2009.pdf.

"It could've been . . . or whoever they were.": Carisa Tomkiel, interview with author. March 22, 2001.

"A large portion . . . talking about football.": Pennsylvania Interbranch Commission (December 7, 2009), p. 369. pacourts.us/Storage/media/pdfs/20210208/162530-dec7,2009.pdf.

"Nope, she has to go now . . . seizure.": Pennsylvania Interbranch Commission (December 7, 2009), p. 372. pacourts.us/Storage/media/pdfs/20210208/162530-dec7,2009.pdf.

"You guys . . . every one of you.": Andrea Tomkiel, interview with author. March 22, 2001.

CHAPTER 2 — JUST GREED

"Something's wrong . . .": Robert P. Wolensky, Kenneth C. Wolensky, Nicole H. Wolensky, *The Knox Mine Disaster*, (Harrisburg, PA: Commonwealth of Pennsylvania, Pennsylvania Historical and Museum Commission, 1999), p. 2.

"One of these days . . . like rats in a trap.": Robert P. Wolensky, Kenneth C. Wolensky, and Nicole H. Wolensky, *Voices of the Knox Mine Disaster* (Harrisburg, PA: Commonwealth of Pennsylvania, Pennsylvania Historical and Museum Commission, 2005), p. 1.

"The entire region . . . looked the other way.": Matt Birkbeck, *The Quiet Don* (New York: Berkley Books, 2013), pp. 36–37.

"A husband, or son, or father...brought home a corpse": Peter Roberts, *The Anthracite Coal Industry*, (New York: The Macmillan Company, 1901), p. 152. hathitrust.org/cgi/pt?id=mdp.39015006955036&view=1up&sq=214&q1=corpse.

"What the hell they wanted to do . . .": Wolensky, *The Knox Mine Disaster*, p. 106.

"No one really commented . . . you were in big trouble.": Wolensky, *The Knox Mine Disaster*, p. 107.

"[The inspectors] didn't even go inside . . . we went out.": Wolensky, *The Knox Mine Disaster*, p. 109.

"I no more than put my foot . . . Niagara Falls.": Wolensky, *The Knox Mine Disaster*, pp. 9–10.

"Get out, the river broke in.": Wolensky, *Voices of the Knox Mine Disaster*, p. 75.

"Get everybody out . . . buddies are drowned.": Wolensky, *Voices of the Knox Mine Disaster*, p. 75.

"I don't think . . . double-dealing.": Wolensky, *Voices of the Knox Mine Disaster*, p. 145.

"That's all, just greed . . . all the time.": Wolensky, *Voices of the Knox Mine Disaster*, p. 83.

"Owners, bosses, inspectors . . . remain to the present.": Wolensky, *The Knox Mine Disaster*, p. 110.

"It shredded our landscape . . . the cause vanished.": "Editorial: Anthracite Mining Heritage Month Worth Celebrating," *Times Leader,* January 12, 2023. timesleader.com/opinion/1595976/editorial-anthracite-mining-heritage -month-worth-celebrating.

"We were under the thumb . . . political barons.": "Scranton Investigation Evokes Feeling of Deja Vu Probe Comes 10 Years After Indictments in Lackawanna County," *Morning Call*, January 21, 2019.

"All you had to do . . . lung insurance.": Deborah Jerock, interview with author. May 14, 2022.

CHAPTER 3 — INTOLERANCE

"Is she ok? Did she die?": April Jerock, interview with author. April 18, 2022.

"lady parts.": April Jerock, interview with author. April 18, 2022.

"just short of being obnoxious": William Ecenbarger, *Kids for Cash* (New York: New Press, 2012), p. 29.

"It's time for people . . . punished.": Michael R. Sisak, "Ciavarella Portrayed Self as 'Citizen's Judge,' Preached Values," *Standard-Speaker*, January 27, 2009.

"The greatest tool . . . punishment": Ecenbarger, *Kids for Cash*, p. 31.

"The harshest punishment": Ecenbarger, *Kids for Cash*, p. 31.

"If you violate . . . pay dearly.": Ecenbarger, *Kids for Cash*, p. 32.

"I wanted these kids . . . had to deal with me.": Robert May, director, *Kids for Cash* (SenArt Films, 2013), 56:16.

"Everybody loved it.": *Report of the Interbranch Commission on Juvenile Justice* (Philadelphia, PA, May 2010), p. 35. pacourts.us/Storage/media/pdfs/2021 0208/161601-interbranchcommission onjuvenilejustice.pdf.

"always fair and firm . . . makes him so special.": Pennsylvania Interbranch Commission on Juvenile Justice. (October 14, 2009) Public Hearing, statement by Judge Chester Muroski quoting from Nov. 6, 2008, letter to the editor. Transcript, p. 78. secure.pacourts.us/Storage/media/pdfs/2021 0208/162616-oct14,2009.pdf.

"My father was very . . . knocks me out cold.": May, *Kids for Cash*, 57:11–58:20.

"Absolute dump . . . disgrace.": *Report of the Interbranch Commission,* p. 14. pacourts.us/Storage/media /pdfs/20210208/161601-inter branchcommissiononjuvenilejustice.pdf.

"The place is old . . . and rodents.": Michael R. Sisak, "Ex-Judge to Face Accusers,"*Standard Speaker*, February 6, 2011.

CHAPTER 4 — FOUR MEN AND TWO BUILDINGS

"Nobody sees anything . . . talks about anything.": "A Mob City Out Of the 1920s—And a Threat to Lawmen," *Philadelphia Inquirer*, October 23, 1977, p. 17.

"was beaten mercilessly . . . funeral home.": Dave Janofsky, "All apologies: Contrition as corrupt Conahan is sentenced to 17½ years." *Citizens' Voice*, September 24, 2011.

"very very close friends.": Robert May, director, *Kids for Cash* (SenArt Films, 2013), 32:09.

"local man of mystery.": "It's Time For The County To Study, Not Ink The Deal," *Times Leader*, November 14, 2004.

"conniving" and "bombastic.": Betty Roccograndi, "Zeroing In: Hasn't Robert Powell been through enough? You be the judge," *Times Leader*, February 27, 2016. timesleader.com/news/516675/zeroing-in-hasnt -robert-powell-been-through-enough-you-be-the-judge.

"facility for the . . . juveniles.": Jennifer Learn-Andes, "Pittston Township, Pa., Residents Upset by Juvenile Center." *Times Leader*, March 1, 2003.

"Residents still can't believe . . . opposing the center.": Learn-Andes, "Pittston Township," *Times Leader,* Saturday, March 1, 2003.

"This is your lucky . . . gonna pay you one.": May, *Kids for Cash,* 35:15.

"That's one hell of a . . .": Craig R. McCoy, "On the stand, Ciavarella admits much, but insists he took no 'cash for kids,'" *Philadelphia Inquirer*, February 16, 2011.

"I don't need to go to bed . . . not fair to the kids.": Jennifer Learn-Andes, "DETENTION CENTER: Lawsuit Threatened in Facility Use Feud," *Times Leader*, November 21, 2002.

CHAPTER 5 — KIDS FOR CASH

"I want Pennsylvania child care . . . is that clear?": William Ecenbarger, *Kids for Cash* (New York: New Press, 2012), p. 49.

"Who takes a kid . . . I was put in shackles" and "Seventeen years later . . . still have trouble.": Testimony, live hearing, Powell v. Wallace, October 10, 2021 (Harrisburg, PA). Federal District Court Judge Christopher C. Conner hears plaintiff David Wallace via video testimony.

"Conahan began screaming . . . bills to pay": Dave Janoski, "Lokuta: Conahan was courthouse king," *Citizens' Voice*, August 8, 2009.

"Just fill the beds.": Pennsylvania Interbranch Commission on Juvenile Justice. (December 7, 2009) Probation placement officer Tom Lavan, interviewed by Judge Dwayne D. Woodruff. Transcript, p. 320. pacourts.us/Storage/media/pdfs/20210208/162530-dec7,2009.pdf.

"weapon,": Document 1853, summary of harms done, Wallace v. Powell, filed November 5, 2021.

"Propulsion of missiles,": Pennsylvania Interbranch Commission on Juvenile Justice. (December 7, 2009), p. 382.

"weapon of mass destruction.": Sol H. Weiss, attorney, closing arguments, Wallace v, Powell, October 25, 2001.

"I want you to count . . . you're going away.": Powell v. Wallace. Live hearing, Rebecca Hackney via video testimony, October 12, 2021.

"It was just a horrible . . .": "Call to Consider Disparities," *CE Noticias Financieres English*, March 5, 2023. .

"How old are you . . . get him out of here.": William Ecenbarger, *Kids for Cash* (New York: New Press, 2012), p.54.

"Your mommy can't help . . .": Federal District Judge Christopher C. Conner, Memorandum, Wallace v. Powell (August 16, 2022), p. 12. pamd.uscourts.gov/sites/pamd/files/opinions/09v286.pdf.

"Good judge . . . to be re-ignited": Undated letter of Robert Morgans to Ciavarella furnished to author by Susan Morgans, received May 23, 2022.

"How many birds . . . out of my courtroom!": Kelcy Morgans, interview with author. August 30, 2022.

"I'm so sorry . . .": Kelcy Morgans, interview with author. August 30, 2022.

"None of us . . . will it ever?": Kelcy Morgans, interview with author. August 30, 2022.

CHAPTER 6 — KINGDOM OF SILENCE

"extended to reach . . . of the Luzerne County Courthouse.": Leo Strupczewski, "Filing: Conahan Was Luzerne Co. Courthouse 'Boss,'" *Legal Intelligencer*, August 11, 2009. law.com/thelegalintelligencer/almID/1202432921540/.

"did not have to go far": Dave Janoski, "Lokuta: Conahan Was Courthouse King," *Citizens' Voice*, August 8, 2009.

"Steve, we would like to contribute . . . if we do.": Pennsylvania Interbranch Commission on Juvenile Justice. (April 12, 2010) Samuel C. Stretton public testimony, p. 102. pacourts.us/Storage/media/pdfs/20210208/162435-april12,2010.pdf.

CHAPTER 7 — DIVERGENCE

"People would put . . . not fun.": Matthew Samson, interview with author. January 11, 2022.

"supervision, care and rehabilitation . . . minimum amount of time": Federal District Judge Christopher C. Conner, Memorandum, Wallace v. Powell (August 16, 2022), p. 9. pamd.uscourts.gov/sites/pamd/files/opinions/09v286.pdf.

"And then there were . . . high school teacher.": Conner, Memorandum, Wallace v. Powell, p. 17. pamd.uscourts.gov/sites/pamd/files/opinions/09v286.pdf.

"I learned how to become . . . sharpen a toothbrush.": Conner, Memorandum, Wallace v. Powell, p. 17. pamd.uscourts.gov/sites/pamd/files/opinions/09v286.pdf.

"You'll be a cog in a machine . . . selling drugs.": Matthew Samson, interview with author. June 6, 2022.

"I didn't know . . . with a PhD.": Unidentified woman (Stefanie Romanski), interview with author. September 22, 2022.

"It's so silly . . . my little relic, I guess.": April Jerock, interview with author. April 18, 2022.

"I got up . . . my face again.": Elizabeth Habel, interview with author. September 22, 2022.

"So, so many . . . did coming out.": Marie Yaeger, interview with author. March 12, 2021.

"I've never encountered . . . make some money.": Marsha Levick, "Pa Judges Accused of Jailing Kids for Cash," Associated Press via NBC News, February 11, 2009. nbcnews.com/id/wbna29142654.

"Shameless . . . heirs of the superrich.": Mark Guydish, "High-flying Former Judges Foiled—Again," *Times Leader*, August 4, 2009. timesleader.com/archive/1221469/high-flying-former-judges-foiled-again-mark-guydish-opinion.

CHAPTER 8 — VILLAIN OR VICTIM

Michael Conahan. "You know . . . Ciavarella.": Terrie Morgan-Besecker, "Powell: Ex-Jurists Demanded Cash," *Times Leader*, February 10, 2011.

"He blew through . . . and thoughtless.": Michael Consiglio, interview with the author. November 3, 2022.

"Don't tell me. . . . burned through it.": Federal Prosecutor Gordon Zubrod to jury, quoted by Zack Needles, "Ciavarella's Federal Racketeering Trial Begins in Scranton," *Legal Intelligencer*, February 9, 2011.

"You've been very. . . . in on it.": "Trial update: Powell's testimony to continue Thursday," *Citizens' Voice*, February 9, 2011.

"two most powerful men . . . with both of them.": Terrie Morgan-Besecker, "Powell: Judges 'two most powerful men' in county," *Times Leader*, February 11, 2011.

"The lion was out of the cage . . . ": Craig R. McCoy, "Witness tells of supplying two Luzerne County Judges with cash," *Philadelphia Inquirer*, February 11, 2011.

"They were absolutely relentless.": Craig R. McCoy, "Ordeal of getting 2 judges the cash; In the Luzerne scandal trial, a lawyer and his staffer told about cramming $100s and $50s into a box and cursing," *Philadelphia Inquirer*, February 13, 2011.

"I'm not doing this anymore . . . ": Craig R. McCoy, "Ordeal of getting 2 judges the cash; In the Luzerne scandal trial, a lawyer and his staffer told about cramming $100s and $50s into a box and cursing," *Philadelphia Inquirer*, February 13, 2011.

"If you can take your children. . . . pay us.": Prosecutor Gordon Zubrod to jury, quoted by Zack Needles, "Ciavarella's Federal Racketeering Trial Begins in Scranton," *Legal Intelligencer*, February 9, 2011.

"These greedy bastards . . . will be over": Craig R. McCoy, "Ordeal of getting 2 judges the cash; In the Luzerne scandal trial, a lawyer and his staffer told about cramming $100s and $50s into a box and cursing," *Philadelphia Inquirer*, February 13, 2011.

"This is the last one . . . the last one.": "On the witness stand: A week in review," *Citizen's Voice*, February 12, 2011.

CHAPTER 9 — STANDING UP

"I'll never do it again . . . going to have one.": Michael McNarney, "Superior Court Overturns Ruling In Child's Case, Judge Mark A. Ciavarella Should Not Have Found A Boy Delinquent In A 1999 Case, The Court Says," *Times Leader*, January 6, 2001.

"an Army surplus . . . patch of sand.": Mark Guydish, "Nature's Boot Camp," *Times Leader,* May 17, 2004. timesleader.com/archive/1060134/natures-boot-camp.

"bombastic" and "loose cannon": Erin Moody, "County Watchdog Flood Dies," *Standard-Speaker*, July 18, 2011.

"It is a bad deal . . . get to pay": Dave Janoski and Jennifer Learn-Andes, "State: County Blundered In Leasing 'Juvie' Center; Documents Question Costs," *Times Leader*, December 22, 2004.

"drivel": Jennifer Learn-Andes, "Flood: Judge's argument is 'drivel'; Juvie center case," *Times Leade*r, November 30, 2005.

"a tremendous amount of money": Jennifer Learn-Andes, "Judge's' letter shocks officials; Commissioner Skrepenak says no one informed him of problems in youth services," *Times Leader*, June 23, 2005.

"Because he tries . . . absolutely furious.": Jennifer Learn-Andes, "Social Worker Blasts Muroski Move; She Praises The Judge And Says Moving Him Was A Mistake," *Times Leader*, May 25, 2005.

"very astute . . . very, very wrong move": Jennifer Learn-Andes, "Social Worker Blasts Muroski Move," *Times Leader,* May 25, 2005.

CHAPTER 10 — CRACKS

"Hello . . . Oh la la!": Robert May, director, *Kids for Cash* (SenArt Films, 2013), 12:20.

"What makes you think . . . you're gone.": William Ecenbarger, *Kids for Cash* (New York: New Press, 2012), pp. 136–138.

"It's ok, it's ok.": May, *Kids for Cash*, 13:44.

"Look what you did to your mother.": May, *Kids for Cash*, 13:58.

"unreasonable": Terrie Morgan-Besecker, "Auditor: County could have built 3 juvie centers." *Times Leader,* January 12, 2008.

"really really . . . red flags.": May, *Kids for Cash*, 16:00.

"I wanted to go . . . Please look at this'.": May, *Kids for Cash*, 16:23

"Nothing is done . . . child gets placed": Michael R. Sisak, "Ciavarella defends county juvie system," *Citizens' Voice*, May 13, 2008.

"I just don't believe . . . things in their life.": Michael R. Sisak, "Ciavarella admits he handled county juvenile cases improperly," *Citizens' Voice*, May 29, 2008.

"shocked and absolutely upset": Dave Janoski, "Skrepenak, Vonderheid unaware of juvenile facility firms' links," *Citizens' Voice*, June 12, 2008.

"A week-long ethics . . . ": Bill O'Boyle, "Activist, giant pig target courthouse: Gene Stilp mocks the Luzerne County building's 100th anniversary celebration." *Times Leader*, September 26, 2009.

CHAPTER 11 — CAT AND MOUSE

"Every time you turn over one rock . . . crawl out.": (Pennsylvania Crime Commission head Frederick Martins) Terrie Morgan-Besecker, "Corruption County," *Times Leader*, December 27, 2009.

"Then we see . . . hiding something here.": Michael Consiglio: interview with the author. November 3, 2022.

"They indicated . . . situation better.": Michael Consiglio, interview with the author. November 3, 2022.

"Bobby, you've got to . . . never came to us.": Dave Janoski and Michael R. Sisak, "Powell recounts judges' pressure to deliver cash," *Citizens' Voice*, February 11, 2011.

"So what are you saying . . . we'll do it.": "In their own words," *Standard-Speaker*, May 13, 2010.

"Listen . . . she has them.": "In their own words," *Standard-Speaker,* May 13, 2010.

"We could actually hear . . . unsuccessful": William Ecenbarger, *Kids for Cash* (New York: New Press, 2012), pp. 195–196.

"I don't have . . . this is over.": Craig R. McCoy, "Ordeal of getting 2 judges the cash: In the Luzerne scandal trial, a lawyer and his staffer told about cramming $100s and $50s into a box and cursing," *Philadelphia Inquirer*, February 13, 2011.

CHAPTER 12 — TERRIBLE, HORRIBLE, NO GOOD

"terrible horrible . . .": Dave Janoski, "Tarnished." *Citizens' Voice*, February 13, 2009.

"Yes, your honor . . . guilty, your honor": Janoski, "Tarnished." *Citizens' Voice*. February 13, 2009.

"Where's the robe at . . . Burn in hell.": Michael R. Sisak, "Parents and juveniles watch for justice in judges' pleas," *Citizens' Voice*, February 13, 2009.

"I hope the Aryan . . . you pigs": Edward Lewis, "Emotions fly outside courthouse," *Times Leader*, February 13, 2009.

"Imagine learning . . . is totally slanted.": Michael Consiglio, with the author. November 3, 2022.

CHAPTER 13 — RAGE AND SORROW

"It was nice . . . side of the bench.": mother (Susan Mishanski), Ian Urbina and Sean D. Hamill, "Judges Plead Guilty in Scheme to Jail Youths for Profit," *New York Times*, February 12, 2009. nytimes.com/2009/02/13/us/13judge.html.

"He sat there . . . the criminal.": mother (Flo Wallace), Sisak, "Parents and juveniles," *Citizens' Voice*. February 13, 2009.

"Then there was me . . . stabbed my mom.": "Their stories," *Citizens' Voice*, February 22, 2009.

"Your honor . . . strict probation.": Elizabeth Habel, interview with author. August 17, 2022.

"She didn't see any light . . . running away.": Pennsylvania Interbranch Commission on Juvenile Justice. (December 7, 2009) Testimony of "G.H." Transcript, pp. 437–438. pacourts.us/Storage/media/pdfs/20210208 /162530-dec7,2009.pdf.

"I [heart] you . . . My Loving Family.": Drawing shared with author by Gloria Habel, September 16, 2022.

"It does not matter . . . my courtroom.": Pennsylvania Interbranch Commission (December 7, 2009), p. 441. pacourts.us/Storage/media/ pdfs/20210208/162530-dec7,2009.pdf.

"They did not switch . . . was hysterical.": Pennsylvania Interbranch Commission (December 7, 2009), p. 441. pacourts.us/Storage/media/ pdfs/20210208/162530-dec7,2009.pdf.

"Whoa, whoa . . . what hearing?": Pennsylvania Interbranch Commission (December 7, 2009), p. 443. pacourts.us/Storage/media/pdfs/20210208 /162530-dec7,2009.pdf.

"He said, 'Do not saying anything . . . exact words to us.": Dave Janoski, Family Fought Back," *Citizens' Voice*, March 1, 2009.

"Elizabeth, I know . . . the last laugh.": Dave Janoski, "Family fought Back," *Citizens' Voice*, March 1, 2009.

CHAPTER 14 — DEAL OR NO DEAL

"Cash for Kids," ABC News *20/20*, June 18, 2009. YouTube. Ciavarella: "Hang on . . .": Avila: "You know . . ." 3:11; Ciavarella: "I'm not pleading guilty . . .": 3:50; Ciavarella, "That's not true . . .": 4:01; Ciavarella, "You take a look . . . like you to think": 4:35; Grim, "You have no business . . . based on the facts": 5:54; Grim, "The kids were . . . is incorrect": 5:00; Grim, "It's kids . . . a bad lesson": 7:53. youtube.com/watch?v=Jdhsf1u3JVY&t=314s.

"According to him . . . laughed about it.": Leo Strupczewski, "Witnesses Tie Reputed Mobster to Luzerne Judge; Security Guard Says She Passed Envelopes; Admitted Felon Describes Meetings," *Legal Intelligencer*, July 2, 2009.

"On several occasions . . . positive for Joseph": Dave Janoski, "Associate: D'Elia, Conahan met often," *Citizens' Voice*, February 27, 2009.

"The words poured out . . . that I was entitled to.": Michael R. Sisak, "Former judge Ciavarella's trial begins Monday," *Standard-Speaker*, February 5, 2011.

"Tellingly . . . best witnesses.": Judge William H. Platt, *Report of the Pennsylvania Interbranch Commission on Juvenile Justice*, p. 16. pacourts. us/Storage/media/pdfs/20210208/161601-interbranchcommissionon juvenilejustice.pdf.

"We paraphrase . . . well after this case.": Hank Grezlak and Leo Strupczewski, "Former Luzerne County Judges Withdraw Their Guilty Please," *Legal Intelligencer*, August 25, 2009.

CHAPTER 15 — DEPTHS OF INDIFFERENCE

"The man you're describing . . . them into college.": Pennsylvania Interbranch Commission on Juvenile Justice. (December 7, 2009) Transcript, p. 310. pacourts.us/Storage/media/pdfs/20210208/162530-dec7,2009.pdf.

"Luzerne County was a . . . their role in them.": Pennsylvania Interbranch Commission on Juvenile Justice. (January 21, 2010) Transcript, pp. 72–87. pacourts.us/Storage/media/pdfs/20210208/162512-jan21,2010.pdf.

"I think community . . . disadvantaged community.": Marsha Levick, interview with author. September 19, 2022.

"How do you feel . . . concerning her son": "Ciavarella Speaks After Verdict," *Times Leader* video, February 18, 2011. YouTube, 0:18–2:54. youtube.com/watch?v=QCExlbGTX_M&t=38s.

CHAPTER 16 — FRISBEE, YOGA, SPIN

"Grave danger . . . from the virus.": James Halpin, "Conahan seeks 'compassionate release' due to pandemic," *Citizens' Voice*, June 10, 2020. citizensvoice.com/conahan-seeks-compassionate-release-due-to-pandemic/article_8430406c-f97c-5eb9-a6e6-b074e65f01be.html.

"There is no reason . . . can't believe it": Chris Kelly, "No justice for Fonzo with Conahan relaxing seaside," *Standard-Speaker*, June 28, 2020.

"duffel bags of cash . . . Switzerland . . . opportunity": Jennifer Learn-Andes, "How big of a payday will Powell get?" *Times Leader*, February 21, 2016.

"All I had to do . . . permeate the community.": Michael Consiglio, interview with the author. November 3, 2022.

"persisted in downplaying . . . he should have.": Federal District Judge Christopher C. Conner decision, US District Court for the Middle District of Pennsylvania, U.S. v. Mark A. Ciavarella, January 14, 2021, p. 4. pahome page.com/wp-content/uploads/sites/91/2021/01/09cr272-Order.pdf.

CHAPTER 17 — UNIMAGINABLE BRUTALITY

"That's it? . . . your story is remarkable.": Testimony, live hearing, Powell v. Wallace, October 10, 2021 (Harrisburg, PA). Federal District Court Judge Christopher C. Conner hears plaintiff Rebecca Hackney.

"None of them . . . toll on me": Powell v. Wallace. Conner hears from plaintiff Dennis Fisher.

"My situation now . . . my life has led.": Powell v. Wallace. Conner hears from plaintiff Robert Benussi.

"No one wanted . . . life got nowhere.": Powell v. Wallace. Conner hears from plaintiff Barroom Stallings.

"Beat up by staff . . . eat bugs," p. 17; "walked on ice . . . bare skin," p. 22; "Bleeding from shackles . . . an animal," p. 23; "held down . . . six hours once," p. 14. Summary of harms, Document 1853, Wallace v. Powell, filed November 5, 2021.

"an asthma attack . . . sprained ankle": Federal District Judge Christopher C. Conner decision, Wallace v. Powell, August 16, 2022, p. 19. pamd.uscourts .gov/sites/pamd/files/opinions/09v286.pdf.

"One guy walked into . . . he put her away.": Max Mitchell, "'Multitudes of Unimaginable Stories': Attorney Talks Strategies for Leading 300-Witness 'Kids-for-Cash' Civil Suit to $206M Verdict." *Legal Intelligencer*, August 24, 2022.

"I watched an . . . he said no.": Live testimony of Elizabeth Lorenz Wallace v. Powell, October 25, 2021.

"shockingly high number": Closing argument, Sol Weiss, Wallace v. Powell, October 25, 2021.

"My father . . . as a result.": Testimony, live hearing, Powell v. Wallace. Conner hears from plaintiff Vincent Burgio.

"Completed sixth grade . . . Temple University.": 32-page spreadsheet, Document 1853, Wallace v. Powell, filed November 5, 2021. p. 18.

"You will graduate . . . bodies for a dollar sign.": Ryan Lamoreaux, interview with author. August 23, 2022. Copy of letter sent to author. October 27, 2021.

"Have you ever felt . . . kicked and punched in the face": Testimony and written statement, Ryan Lamoreaux, Wallace v. Powell, provided to author October 27, 2021.

CHAPTER 18 — HARM REDUCTION

"E., do you have . . . not following others.": Newark Youth Court, witnessed live by the author, via Zoom, June 14, 2022.

"The research . . . as they mature.": Liz Ryan, interview with Nicole Ellis, *PBS NewsHour*, April 4, 2023. pbs.org/newshour/nation/how-the-top-u-s -official-for-incarcerated-youth-sees-the-challenges-for-kids-in-the-justice -system.

"When people are incarcerated . . . completely disrupted.": Elizabeth Kauffman, interview with the author. September 22, 2022.

"I apologize . . . for more growth.": Lilly Nguyen, "In Orange County, Young Adult Court offers a path to clear felony convictions," *Los Angeles Times*, January 25, 2021. latimes.com/california/story/2021-01-25/graduates -emerge-felony-free-from-orange-county-young-adult-court.

"I know other kids . . . stay on track.": Carisa Tomkiel, interview with author. November 14, 2022.

CHAPTER 19 — BRANDED

"What are we doing . . . here for toys.": Matthew Samson, interview with author. July 24, 2022.

"Why would they . . . did you do": Matthew Samson, interview with author. January 11, 2022.

"Hey Bad Matthew . . . I must be bad.": Matthew Samson, interview with author. January 11, 2022.

"Thank God . . .[expletive] LOVE you.": Stefanie Romanski, interview with author. September 22, 2022.

"Their reputation . . . harm is far-reaching.": Judge Christopher C. Conner, live closing arguments, Wallace v. Powell, November 18, 2021 (Wilkes-Barre, PA).

"I was labeled.": Federal District Judge Christopher C. Conner, Memorandum, Wallace v. Powell (August 16, 2022), p. 23. pamd.uscourts.gov/sites/pamd/files/opinions/09v286.pdf.

"The backlash . . . about the past.": Carisa Tomkiel, interview with author. March 22, 2021.

"Coaches didn't want . . . on their team.": Federal District Judge Christopher C. Conner, Memorandum, Wallace v. Powell (August 16, 2022), p. 23. pamd.uscourts.gov/sites/pamd/files/opinions/09v286.pdf.

"like little gangsters": April Jerock, interview with author. April 18, 2022.

"They were garnishing . . . there was something.": Deborah Jerock, interview with author. July 30, 2022.

"Although most memories . . . stories are never forgotten.": Federal District Judge Christopher C. Conner decision, Wallace v. Powell (August 16, 2022), pp. 1, 10, 40. uscourts.gov/sites/pamd/files/opinions/09v286.pdf.

"If I could take . . . with commas ever could.": Ryan Lamoreaux, interview with author. August 23, 2022.

"You get branded . . . definitely my rock.": Matthew Samson, interview with author. June 6, 2022.

INDEX

Page numbers in boldface refer to images and/or captions.

IMAGE CREDITS